INTERNATIONAL DEVELOPMENT IN FOCUS

Spatial Analysis of Liberia's Transport Connectivity and Potential Growth

Atsushi Iimi and Kulwinder Rao

© 2018 International Bank for Reconstruction and Development / The World Bank
1818 H Street NW, Washington, DC 20433
Telephone: 202-473-1000; Internet: www.worldbank.org

Some rights reserved

1 2 3 4   21 20 19 18

Books in this series are published to communicate the results of Bank research, analysis, and operational experience with the least possible delay. The extent of language editing varies from book to book.

This work is a product of the staff of The World Bank with external contributions. The findings, interpretations, and conclusions expressed in this work do not necessarily reflect the views of The World Bank, its Board of Executive Directors, or the governments they represent. The World Bank does not guarantee the accuracy of the data included in this work. The boundaries, colors, denominations, and other information shown on any map in this work do not imply any judgment on the part of The World Bank concerning the legal status of any territory or the endorsement or acceptance of such boundaries.

Nothing herein shall constitute or be considered to be a limitation upon or waiver of the privileges and immunities of The World Bank, all of which are specifically reserved.

Rights and Permissions

This work is available under the Creative Commons Attribution 3.0 IGO license (CC BY 3.0 IGO) http://creativecommons.org/licenses/by/3.0/igo. Under the Creative Commons Attribution license, you are free to copy, distribute, transmit, and adapt this work, including for commercial purposes, under the following conditions:

Attribution—Please cite the work as follows: Iimi, Atsushi, and Kulwinder Rao. 2018. *Spatial Analysis of Liberia's Transport Connectivity and Potential Growth*. International Development in Focus. Washington, DC: World Bank. doi:10.1596/978-1-4648-1286-6 License: Creative Commons Attribution CC BY 3.0 IGO

Translations—If you create a translation of this work, please add the following disclaimer along with the attribution: *This translation was not created by The World Bank and should not be considered an official World Bank translation. The World Bank shall not be liable for any content or error in this translation.*

Adaptations—If you create an adaptation of this work, please add the following disclaimer along with the attribution: *This is an adaptation of an original work by The World Bank. Views and opinions expressed in the adaptation are the sole responsibility of the author or authors of the adaptation and are not endorsed by The World Bank.*

Third-party content—The World Bank does not necessarily own each component of the content contained within the work. The World Bank therefore does not warrant that the use of any third-party-owned individual component or part contained in the work will not infringe on the rights of those third parties. The risk of claims resulting from such infringement rests solely with you. If you wish to re-use a component of the work, it is your responsibility to determine whether permission is needed for that re-use and to obtain permission from the copyright owner. Examples of components can include, but are not limited to, tables, figures, or images.

All queries on rights and licenses should be addressed to World Bank Publications, The World Bank Group, 1818 H Street NW, Washington, DC 20433, USA; e-mail: pubrights@worldbank.org.

ISBN: 978-1-4648-1286-6
DOI: 10.1596/978-1-4648-1286-6

Cover photo: © Infrastructure Implementation Unit, Republic of Liberia. Used with permission; further permission required for reuse.
Cover design: Debra Naylor / Naylor Design Inc.

Contents

About the Authors   vii
Executive Summary   ix
Abbreviations   xxv

CHAPTER 1: **Introduction**   1
    Notes   5
    References   6

CHAPTER 2: **The Current Road Network**   7
    Roads   7
    Bridges and Culverts   9
    Climate Vulnerability   12
    Notes   15
    References   15

CHAPTER 3: **Domestic Connectivity**   17
    Rural Accessibility   17
    Market Accessibility   22
    Access to a Port   24
    Possible Opportunities to Develop Cabotage   31
    Access to Social Facilities   35
    Notes   40
    References   41

CHAPTER 4: **Broader Transport Connectivity**   43
    Intermodal Connectivity   43
    Regional Connectivity   47
    Note   50
    Reference   50

CHAPTER 5: **Potential Economic and Social Benefits from Improved Connectivity**   51
    Agricultural Production   51
    Fisheries   54
    Firm Agglomeration   57
    Social Benefits: Health Care Access   60
    Potential Trip Delay Costs Caused by Road Flooding   61
    Notes   64
    References   65

CHAPTER 6: **Financial Requirements and Further Works** 69
Tentative Financial Requirement Estimates 69
Possible Partnership with Concessionaires for Road Investment and Maintenance 73
Future Works 80
Notes 81
Reference 81

CHAPTER 7: **Conclusion** 83

Appendix A: **Global Experience of Cabotage** 87

Appendix B: **Public-Private Partnership Framework and Case Studies in Liberia** 93

Box
3.1 Global Experiences with Vessel Registration and Cabotage 35

Figures
ES.1 Liberian growth remains weak, fluctuating, and vulnerable to external shocks x
ES.2 Most paved roads are well maintained, but nearly 60 percent of unpaved roads are in poor condition xi
ES.3 Road structures are critical, nearly half of bridges and one-quarter of culverts are in poor condition xi
ES.4 Access to higher level of health care services is a challenge xiv
ES.5 More crops are produced where proximity to domestic markets, especially Monrovia, is high xvii
ES.6 The firm distribution is more skewed than the population distribution xx
ES.7 Better transport infrastructure can help improve people's access to health care services xx
1.1 Liberia: gross domestic product growth rate 2
1.2 Annual crop yield 2
1.3 Urbanization rate 3
1.4 Rural population 4
1.5 Government expenditures on road development 5
2.1 Road density 8
2.2 Liberia's road condition according to surface type 10
2.3 Percentage of roads in poor condition 11
2.4 Condition of bridges and culverts 11
3.1 Absolute poverty rate 20
3.2 Poverty and rural accessibility 21
3.3 Types of commodities passing through freeport of Monrovia, 2014 25
3.4 Port traffic of selected ports in West Africa 26
3.5 Port performance indicators at selected African ports 27
3.6 Africa: imports and economic growth 27
3.7 Share of population according to port access 31
3.8 Share of population with health care access 38
5.1 Major crop production 52
5.2 Transport costs to market and crop production value 53
5.3 Market access index and crop production value 53
5.4 Correlation between rural access index and crop production 54
5.5 Fishery production, 2014 55
5.6 Fishery trade volume, 2013 55
5.7 Correlation between number of crews and market access 57
5.8 Geographic concentration in Liberia 58
5.9 Health care access and transport connectivity 61
5.10 Road fragility curve 63
6.1 Government revenues from extractive industry 74
6.2 Share of concessions, 2014 77
A.1 SSS share in the cargo movement in Brazil, 1998–2010 88

Maps

ES.1 First-ever georeferenced road inventory survey was carried out, with 11,423 km of roads surveyed   x
ES.2 Approximately 12 percent of Liberia's roads are exposed to flood risk   xii
ES.3 Only 42 percent of rural populations have access to the road network   xiii
ES.4 Market accessibility is a challenge beyond the Monrovia area and Monrovia-Ganta corridor   xiv
ES.5 Connecting health facilities to Monrovia is important   xv
ES.6 Significant transport cost reduction is expected by developing cabotage between Monrovia and other ports   xvi
ES.7 Fishery has potential, but local landing sites are not connected to markets   xviii
ES.8 In Liberia, economic activities, especially firms, are highly concentrated around Monrovia   xix
1.1 Population distribution and road network   3
2.1 Liberia's road network condition, 2016   9
2.2 Bridges: location and condition   12
2.3 Culverts: location and condition   13
2.4 Flood-prone areas and road network   14
3.1 Rural access index, 2016   18
3.2 Recent major World Bank-financed road improvement projects   19
3.3 Poverty headcount by county, 2016   20
3.4 Change in poverty rate between 2014 and 2016   21
3.5 Transport costs to market   22
3.6 Market access index   24
3.7 Transport costs to Freeport of Monrovia   28
3.8 Transport costs to four major ports   29
3.9 Change in transport costs taking Buchanan, Greenville, and Harper into account   30
3.10 Location of health facilities   37
3.11 Key routes from Monrovia to hospitals   38
3.12 Health facility connectivity to Monrovia   39
3.13 Key routes from districts to hospitals   40
4.1 Transport costs to Monrovia with cabotage   44
4.2 Reduction in transport costs with cabotage   45
4.3 Transport costs to four major ports with the Lamco rail line taken into account   46
4.4 Reduction in transport costs with Lamco rail line taken into account   47
4.5 Regional access index   49
4.6 Important roads for regional connectivity   50
5.1 Current agricultural production areas   52
5.2 Landing sites and key routes to markets   56
5.3 Number of firms registered by district, 2016   59
5.4 Twenty-five-year flood depth   62
5.5 Transport costs to market under flood scenario   63
5.6 Change in transport costs caused by potential floods   64
6.1 Key areas to promote crop production   72
6.2 Port hinterland to be connected to cover at least 200,000 people   73
6.3 Mining, agriculture, and forestry concession areas   76

Tables

ES.1 Liberia's financial needs estimates by road classification   xxi
ES.2 Liberia's financial needs estimates by development objective   xxii
2.1 Liberia's road network   8
2.2 Results of road inventory survey according to surface type   9
2.3 Thresholds for road condition classification   10
2.4 Result of road inventory survey according to road class   10
2.5 Roads in flood areas   13
2.6 Bridges and culverts in flood-prone areas   14
3.1 Estimated direct beneficiaries   19

3.2	Population with access to markets	23
3.3	Port traffic in Liberia	25
3.4	Port infrastructure	26
3.5	Population with access to a port	30
3.6	Physical characteristics of major ports in Liberia	32
3.7	Number of health facilities mapped	36
3.8	Population with health care access	37
3.9	Priority roads identified for health service accessibility	39
4.1	Transport costs to Monrovia with cabotage	44
4.2	Customs revenue according to customs office, 2014/15	48
4.3	Major commodities trade at border crossings	48
5.1	Condition of key routes from landing sites to markets	56
5.2	Labor statistics in Liberia	58
5.3	Firms registered, 2016	59
6.1	Tentative estimates of financial requirements	70
6.2	Estimated financial requirements by development areas	71
6.3	Government revenues from extractive industry by sector, 2014/15	74
6.4	Concession areas and road length by sector	75
6.5	Major concessions by sector	76
6.6	Recent concession activities approved by PPCC	77
6.7	Basic characteristics of concession frameworks by sector	77
7.1	Summary of opportunities and challenges	84
B.1	Procurement steps by PPC act	99

About the Authors

Atsushi Iimi is a Senior Economist in the Transport and Digital Development Global Practice of the World Bank where he specializes in industrial organization and development economics related to the Bank's transport operations in Africa. He joined the World Bank in 2006 after earning a doctorate in economics from Brown University. Before joining the Bank, he also worked at the International Monetary Fund and Japan International Cooperation Agency/ Overseas Economic Cooperation Fund, Japan. His research interests include spatial analysis, rural accessibility, evaluation of transport and energy projects, growth, and public expenditure. His research on these topics has been published in scholarly journals, such as the *Review of Industrial Organization, Journal of Urban Economics, Journal of Applied Economics, The Developing Economies,* and *IMF Staff Papers.*

Kulwinder Rao is Senior Highway Engineer and Global Lead for Fragile and Conflict-Affected Countries in the Transport and Digital Development Global Practice of the World Bank. He is a professional engineer with over 32 years of experience in highway policy planning, engineering, and project management including performance-based contracting (PBC) methodologies including output and performance-based road contract and public private partnership. His experience includes designing and implementing road concession programs in the state of Punjab, India, leading several large design and building infrastructure projects in the Middle East, and development of PBCs in Liberia, Mozambique, Uganda, Botswana, Bolivia, Sri Lanka, India, and China under Bank-funded projects. Before joining the Bank, he has worked at the highest level in road administration in India and held senior management positions in the private sector. He received a bachelor of science degree (with honors) in civil engineering from Punjab University, India.

Executive Summary

Before the Ebola crisis in 2014, Liberia was experiencing robust economic growth, mainly driven by strong mining activities (figure ES.1). As the economy recovers from the Ebola crisis, significant challenges lie ahead. Agriculture, which is an important sector in Liberia, employing approximately half of the labor force, still has a weak growth trajectory. Many rural farmers are not well connected to markets and live below the poverty line. In addition, the economy is still vulnerable to external shocks, such as international commodity prices and rapid spread of possible infectious diseases. Fiscal balances are likely to deteriorate in the short term.

To use limited resources effectively, strategic planning and prioritization of public investment is essential and more crucial than ever before. The Ebola crisis revealed the vulnerability of the country's transport connectivity and health systems. Climate change is another challenge. Liberia is vulnerable to sea level rise, floods, and heat waves, which are projected to become worse. In 2007, for instance, massive floods damaged transport infrastructure.

The goals of this report are to: (a) Consolidate available spatial and subnational data on Liberia; (b) Examine the country's transport constraints and economic opportunities through a spatial lens; and (c) Analyze the possible effect of improved transport connectivity on the economy.

Road infrastructure. The road network, comprising 11,423 kilometers of roads, is sufficient to cover the entire country, but road quality has long been a matter of concern. Before this report, there was no detailed geo-referenced detailed road network data in Liberia, which was hampering effective road asset management by the road authorities. In May 2016, a nationwide road inventory survey was carried out using a smartphone application. The survey generated the first-ever georeferenced road network data that are considered accurate (map ES.1). More than 90 percent of paved roads are in good or fair condition (figure ES.2), but nearly 60 percent of unpaved roads are in poor or very poor condition. This is one of the main findings revealed by the road inventory survey that was conducted under this study.

x | SPATIAL ANALYSIS OF LIBERIA'S TRANSPORT CONNECTIVITY AND POTENTIAL GROWTH

FIGURE ES.1
Liberian growth remains weak, fluctuating, and vulnerable to external shocks

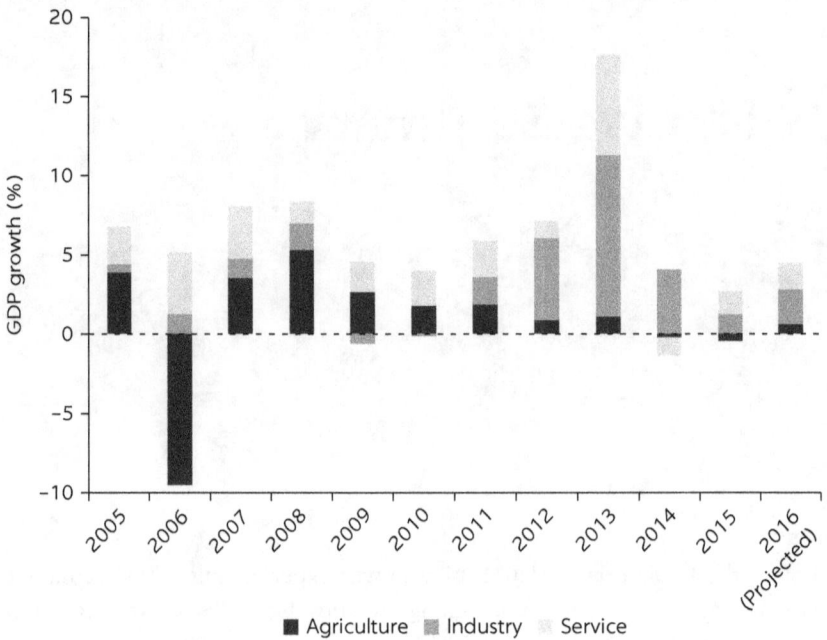

MAP ES.1
First-ever georeferenced road inventory survey was carried out, with 11,423 km of roads surveyed

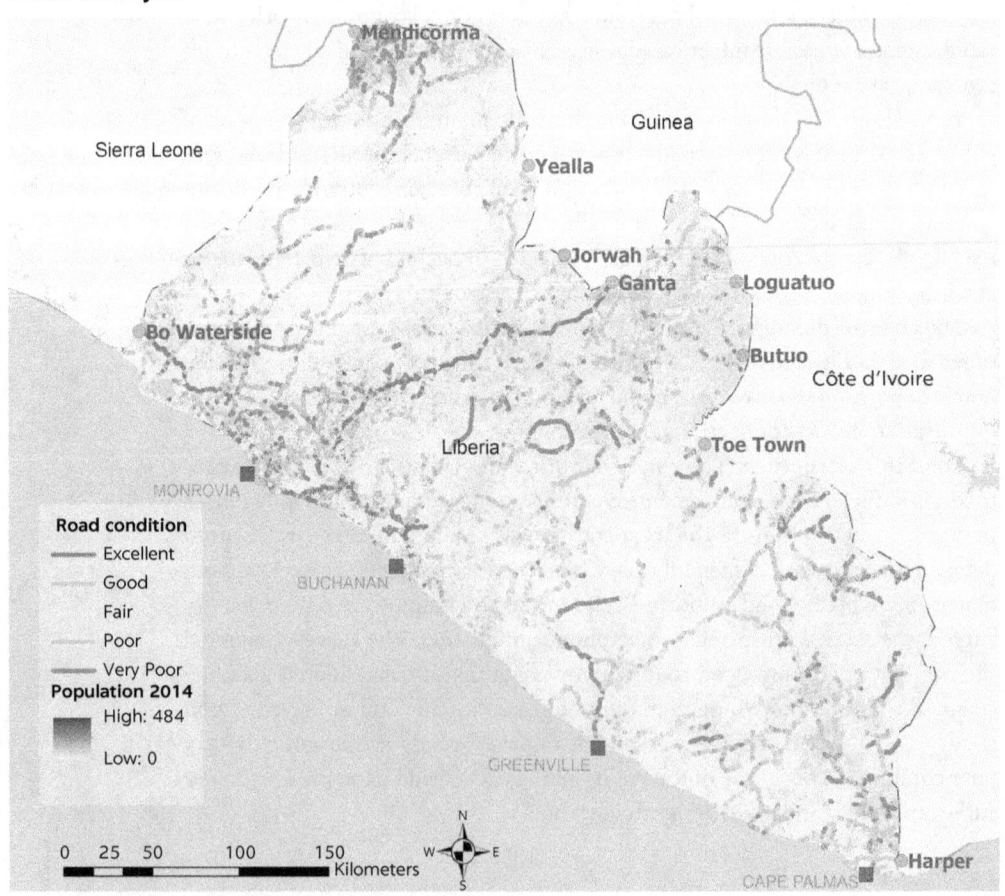

FIGURE ES.2

Most paved roads are well maintained, but nearly 60 percent of unpaved roads are in poor condition

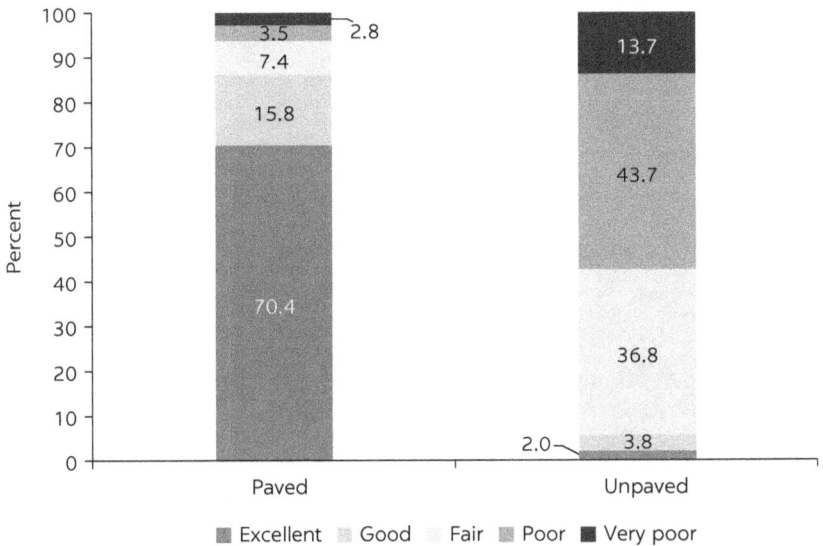

FIGURE ES.3

Road structures are critical, nearly half of bridges and one-quarter of culverts are in poor condition

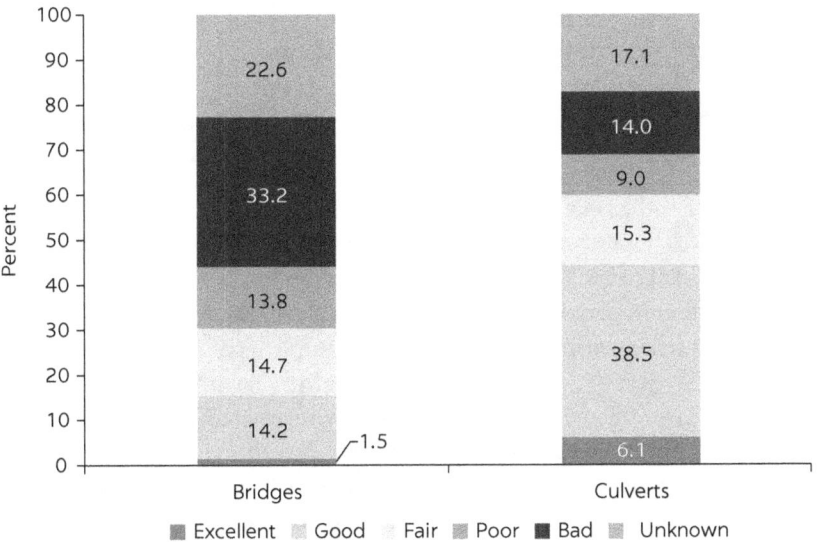

Road structures are crucial for transport connectivity in tropical, humid climates. There are 2,884 bridges and 7,651 culverts in Liberia, but approximately half of the bridges and one-quarter of the culverts are in poor condition, presumably limiting accessibility during the rainy season. Only 15 percent of bridges and half of culverts are in excellent or good condition (figure ES.3).

In addition, Liberia is vulnerable to climate events such as floods, sea level rise, and heat waves. In 2007, exceptionally high rainfall caused floods in West Africa. In Liberia, approximately 12 percent of the road network is in flood-prone areas (map ES.2). Greater attention needs to be paid to this, because floods and downpours can easily wash away unpaved roads that are not properly maintained.

MAP ES.2

Approximately 12 percent of Liberia's roads are exposed to flood risk

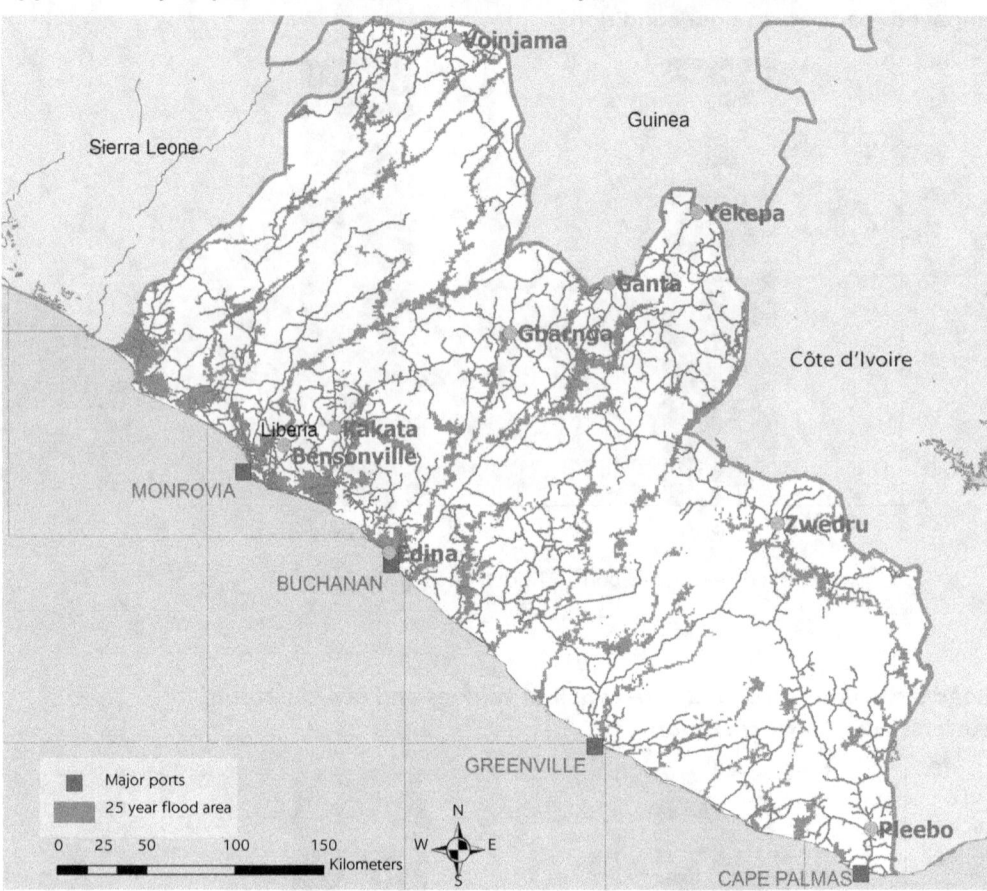

244 bridges and 735 culverts are located in flood-prone areas, but more than two-thirds of these structures are in poor condition, indicating weaknesses of Liberia's road network.

Domestic connectivity. The poor quality of the road network has long been a crucial constraint on mobility in Liberia. The Rural Access Index (RAI), which measures the share of the rural population that lives in within 2 kilometers of a road in good condition, is estimated to be 41.9 percent (map ES.3), meaning that about 2.3 million people are not connected to the good road network. Accessibility varies in different regions. The RAI is particularly low in Lofa County and the southeastern region, where many poor people live, and they have accessibility of less than 10 percent. There is significant correlation between poverty and rural accessibility.

The recent project implemented along the Monrovia–Ganta Corridor and the Monrovia–Buchanan Corridor is estimated to have increased the RAI by 8.4 percent. Although it is a trunk road improvement project, it goes through rural areas, connecting a number of communities along the corridors. Since population density is high in the project area, as many as 400,000 people are estimated to have benefited from the projects, of whom approximately 328,000 are rural residents.

Market accessibility is generally good in Liberia, which is a highly urbanized economy. Approximately 90 percent of the total population is estimated to live within a 2-hour distance from a large city, but beyond Monrovia and the

MAP ES.3

Only 42 percent of rural populations have access to the road network

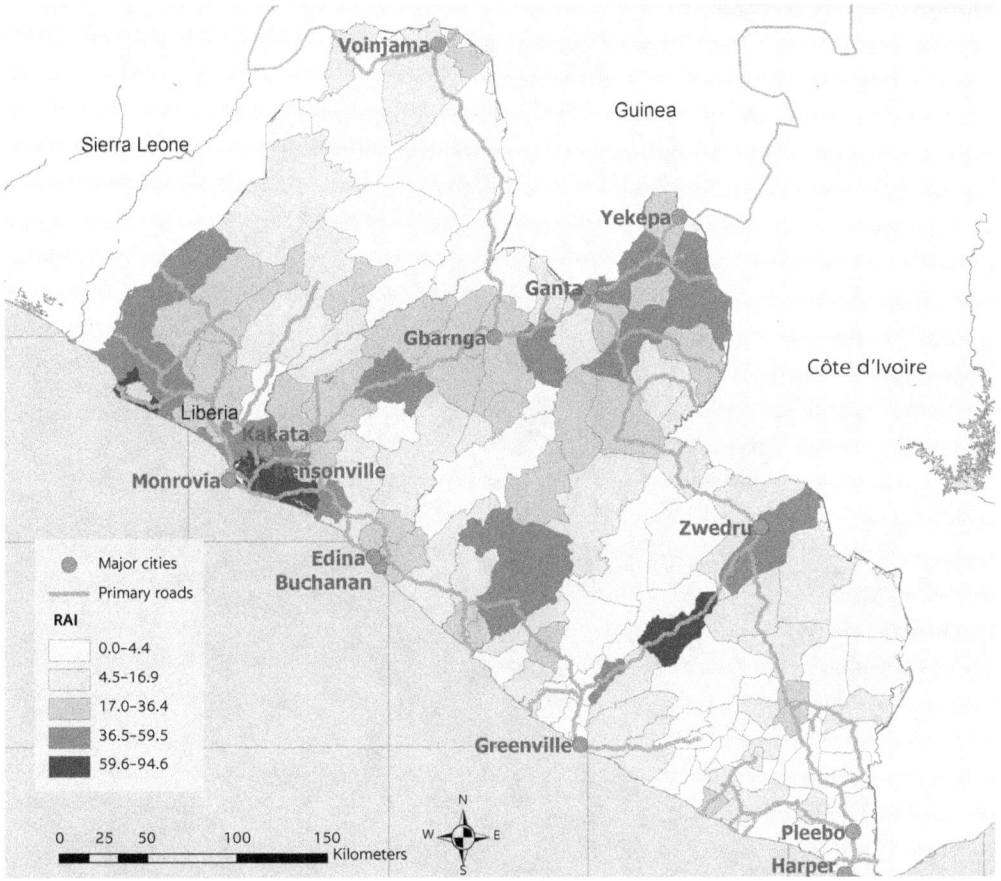

Monrovia–Ganta corridor, market accessibility is a challenge, particularly in Gbapolu, River Cess, and Nimba Counties. Transport costs are estimated to be high (more than US$10 per ton), which makes it difficult for people to get their products to markets and earn a livelihood (map ES.4).

When the size of market is taken into account, the northern and southeastern regions are found completely disconnected from the market of Monrovia, which is much larger than that of other cities. Monrovia has a population of 1.2 million, or one-fourth of the total population. It also has Freeport, the primary port of the country, through which most imports come. The inland connectivity remains a crucial constraint.

Reliable transport infrastructure is also essential to ensure people's connectivity to social facilities, such as health facilities and schools. Many people seem to have access to basic health services at least at the clinic level. People have at least one health facility within 20 kilometers of their home (figure ES.4), but access to the higher level of services that hospitals and health centers provide is difficult.

Connectivity of major health facilities to Monrovia is of particular importance because Liberia's medical supply depends heavily on foreign aid, which often comes through Monrovia. To this end, some 2,600 kilometers of roads are critical, of which approximately 1,100 kilometers are in poor condition and need to be improved (map ES.5). Two-thirds of major health facilities are not connected because of the poor condition of roads.

MAP ES.4

Market accessibility is a challenge beyond the Monrovia area and Monrovia-Ganta corridor

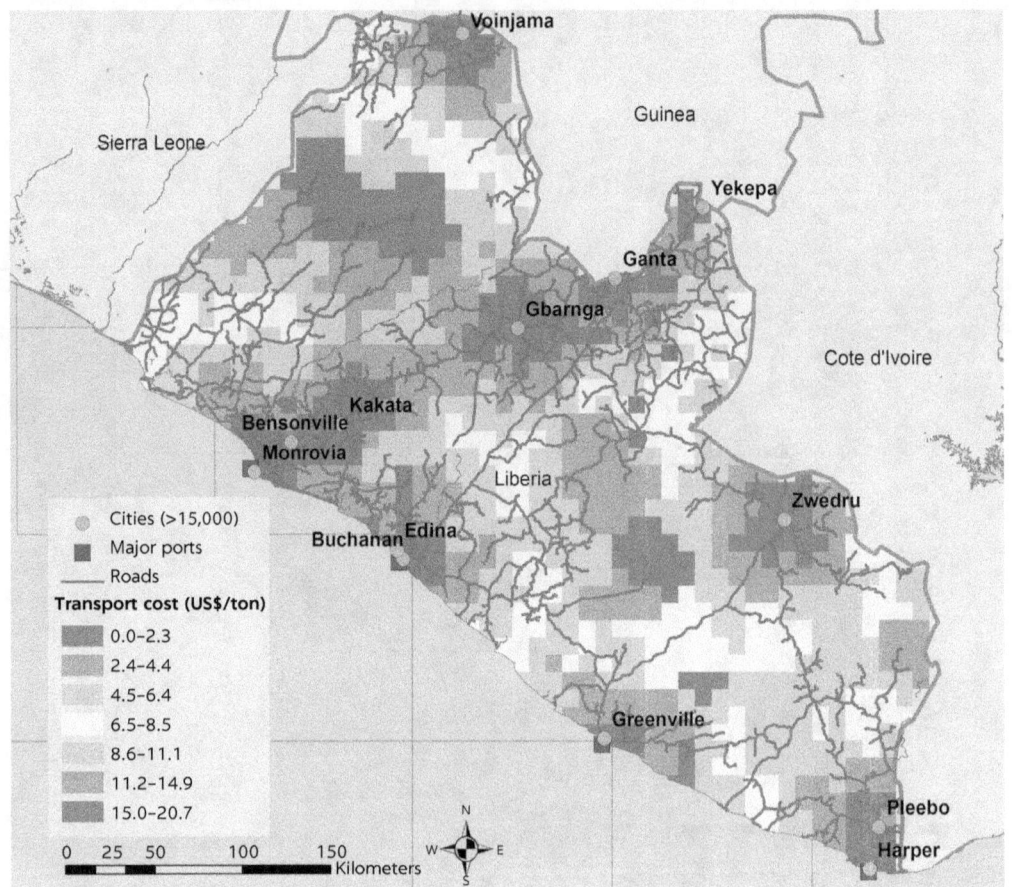

FIGURE ES.4

Access to higher level of health care services is a challenge

MAP ES.5
Connecting health facilities to Monrovia is important

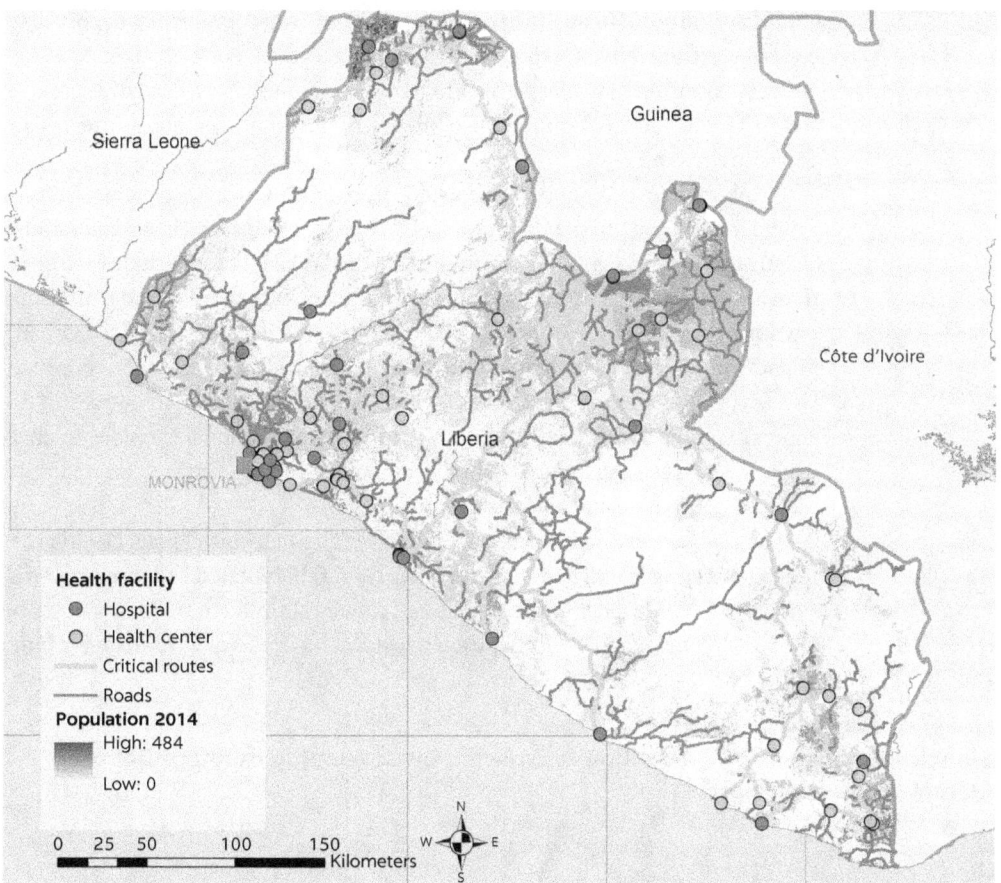

Intermodal and regional connectivity. Good access to ports is essential to improve the productivity of the economy. Seaports are important assets for Liberia. The vast majority of import and export traffic passes through Freeport of Monrovia. In general, port operations exhibit economies of scale, but Freeport of Monrovia is reaching capacity. The average container dwell time is 15 days. Liberia is a significant importing economy. As the economy picks up, it is likely that the demand for port traffic will increase. Port accessibility is relatively good along the Monrovia–Ganta Corridor. Two-thirds of the total population lives 4 hours from the port of Freeport, but transport costs are high for the southeastern regions, such as Pleebo.

Integrated, intermodal transportation through cabotage is one of the possible solutions that are worth evaluating given the fact that Liberia's high urban population lives in the port cities of Monrovia, Buchanan, Greenville, and Harper as well as the limited road transport connectivity in inland areas. Negative externalities of road transport, such as congestion and air pollution, can be reduced if there is a significant modal shift in favor of maritime transport. In addition, maritime transport offers potentially cheaper freight rates than overland or air shipment. Cabotage can be operationalized utilizing existing maritime infrastructure or with little augmentation. There may be potential to develop cabotage at a low cost, especially where existing infrastructure is underutilized.

Cabotage between Freeport and other major ports can improve connectivity between Monrovia the other major coastal cities. Transport costs from Monrovia to Buchanan, Greenville, and Harper could be reduced by up to 80 percent, and the transport distance would be up to 200 kilometers less. Economic benefits could be significant in inland areas of the southeastern counties. Transport costs could be reduced by 10–30 percent over large areas. For instance, cabotage between Monrovia and Harper would reduce shipping costs to Zwedru, the capital of Grand Gedeh County. Of course, efficient and seamless intermodal connectivity is essential.

In Liberia, the current port capacities seem to allow certain developments of cabotage from the physical point of view. However, certain policies and administrative interventions are required or of particular use. These include (a) formation of a maritime administration and safety agency, which governs the maritime law for operation and enforcement of cabotage; (b) formulation of coastal and inland shipping act, which defines the mechanism for applicability of cabotage law; (c) operational waivers for vessels wholly owned or manned or built in the country (in this case, Liberia); and (d) provision of situational variables, such as price incentives that induce switching modes from road to sea, for example, "ecotax" or a rebate on short sea shipping rates.

The railways are another important asset. The Lamco rail line (270 kilometers) connecting Ganta and Buchanan has been rehabilitated and is operational. Compared with road transport, this rail line could reduce transport costs by 20–30 percent (map ES.6). Rail transportation has general advantage for bulk,

MAP ES.6

Significant transport cost reduction is expected by developing cabotage between Monrovia and other ports

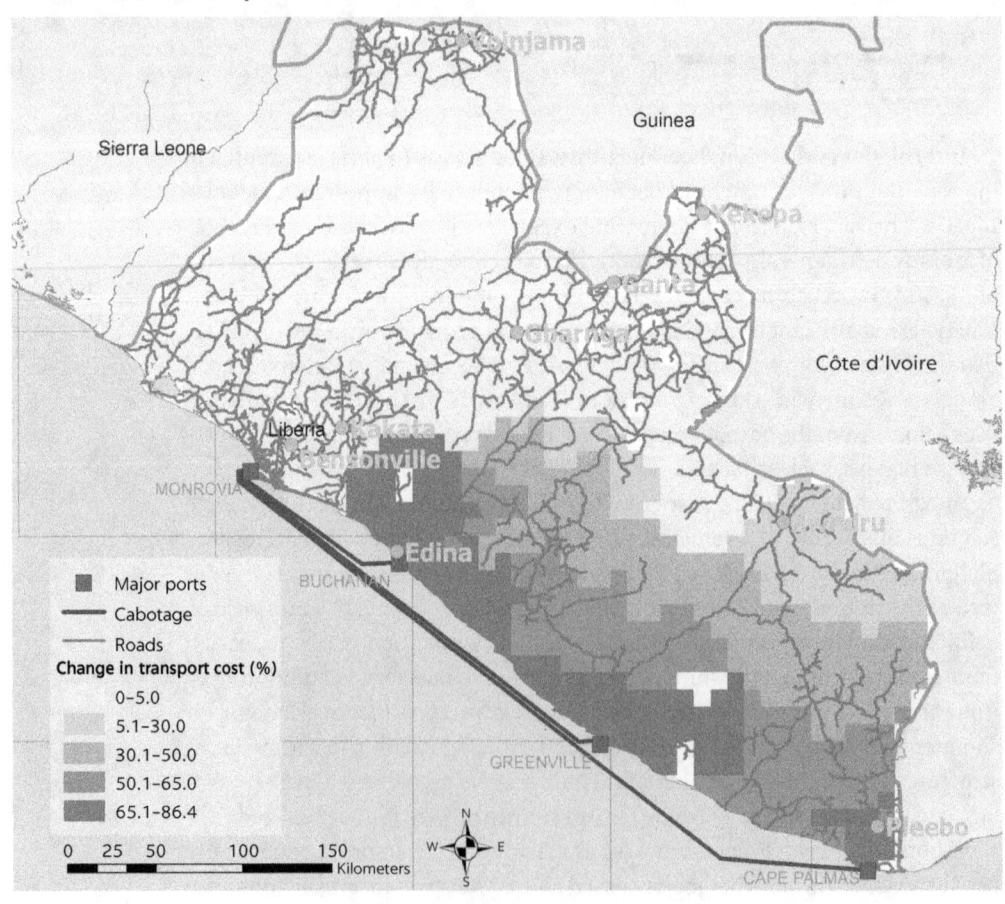

long-haul shipment, possibly including regional freight demand. There is the possibility of developing more regional trade activities in the north central region around Ganta (Bong and Nimba Counties). These areas are relatively well connected to neighboring countries, especially Guinea and Côte d'Ivoire. The Lamco rail line could contribute more to promoting regional integration, if regional inland connectivity is strengthened, especially along the Harper–Voinjama corridor.

Expected benefits from improved connectivity. Agriculture is an important economic sector in Liberia. Approximately half of the population engages in agriculture production, and approximately US$350 million in crops is produced annually. Cassava, sugarcane, and rice are major crops in Liberia. Agricultural production is concentrated around Monrovia and Bong County. The country's agricultural productivity is low. Rural accessibility is necessary to stimulate agricultural production (figure ES.5). Access to markets with purchasing capacity, not just to a city, is particularly important. The correlation with transport costs to a large city is estimated at –0.31. When the size of the population is taken into account, the correlation is higher (0.56 in absolute terms), indicating the importance of Monrovia as a major domestic market.

Fisheries are another important and perhaps untapped potential sector in Liberia. The country has a 570-kilometer-long coastline. Approximately 9,000 crews, including approximately 3,000 foreign fishermen, engage in fishing activities, landing some 7,000 tons of fish per year, yet the country imports approximately 100 tons of fish every year (map ES.7). The estimated production volume of Liberia is far lower than that of neighboring countries.

The regional market seems to have potential. Liberia and its neighboring countries are all fish importers. Because fish are perishable, local connectivity

FIGURE ES.5

More crops are produced where proximity to domestic markets, especially Monrovia, is high

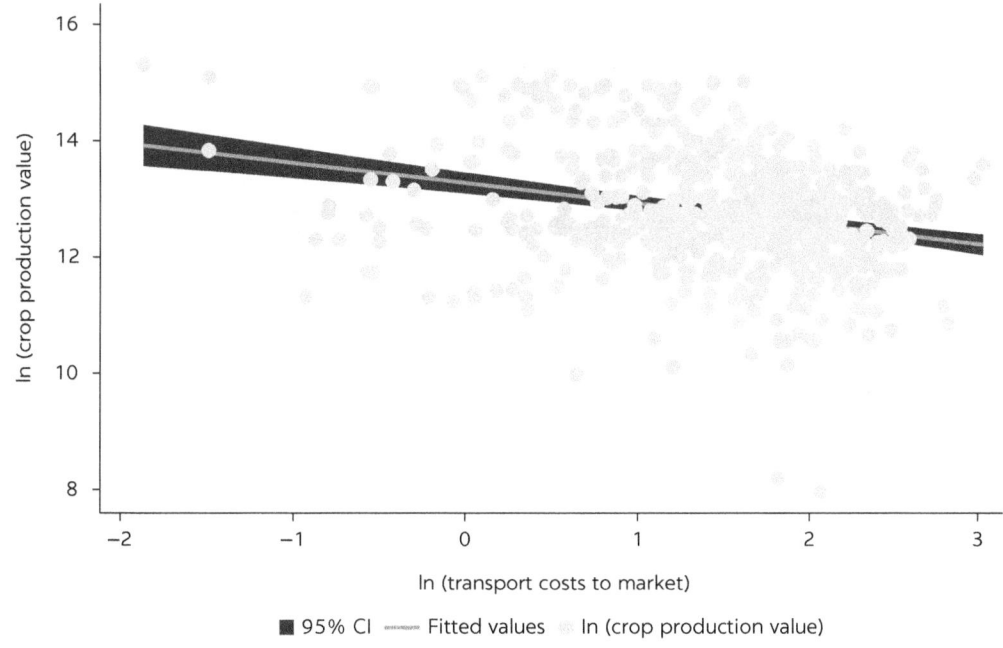

continued

FIGURE ES.5, continued

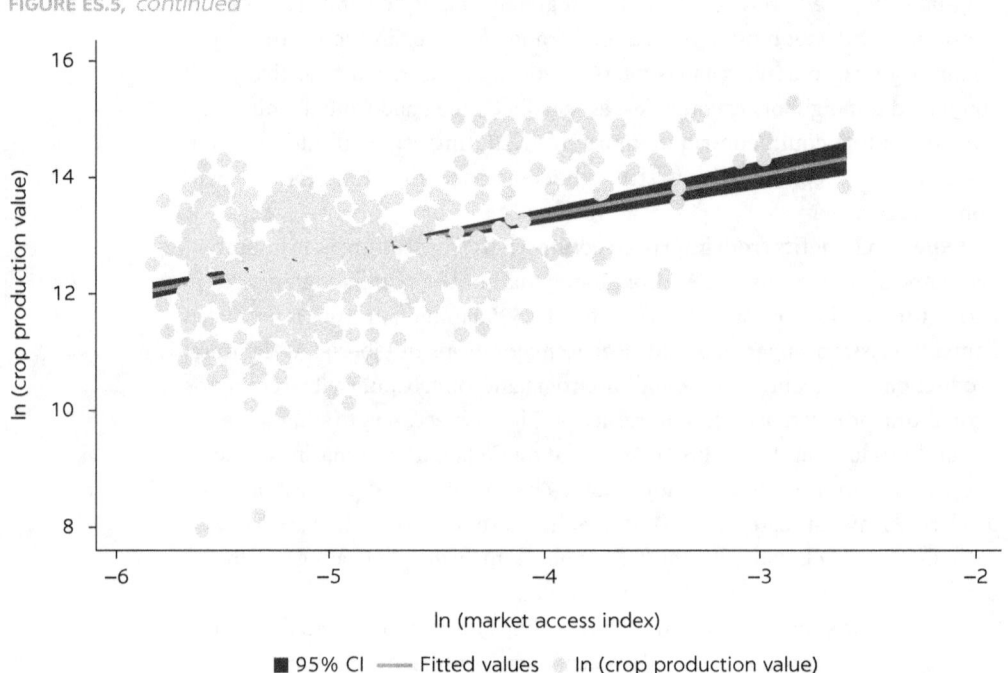

MAP ES.7

Fishery has potential, but local landing sites are not connected to markets

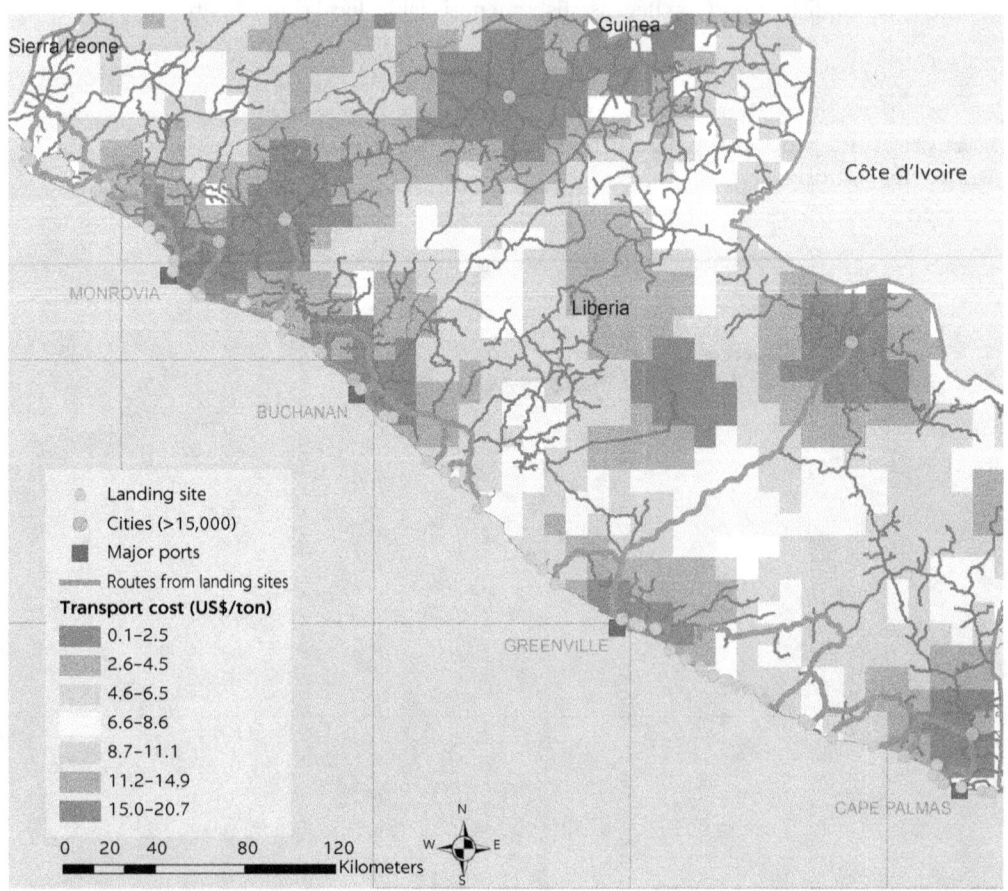

from landing sites to markets is crucial. Most feeder roads are in poor condition. Approximately 1,280 kilometers of roads can be identified as important routes to connect landing sites to markets, out of which about 1,000 kilometers need to be improved and maintained.

In Liberia, economic activities are highly concentrated in Monrovia. More than 41,000 firms were registered in Liberia as of 2016. Approximately 80 percent are located in Montserrado County (map ES.8 and figure ES.6). In general, firms are located where market accessibility is better and where other firms are already established (i.e., agglomeration economies). Although the formal sector remains thin in Liberia, the primary city, Monrovia, is likely to continue to grow and attract more people and firms. This calls for effective long-term urban planning, and perhaps, mass transit development.

Health care access is a challenge in rural Liberia. The health service network looks to cover the entire country, but road connectivity remains a challenge. To enhance access to health care, particularly to the high level of services provided in hospitals, not only rural accessibility but also wider transport connectivity needs to be available. Health care access, measured by the total number of patients who visited each health facility, increases with road density and quality and decreases with transport costs to a market or port (figure ES.7).

MAP ES.8

In Liberia, economic activities, especially firms, are highly concentrated around Monrovia

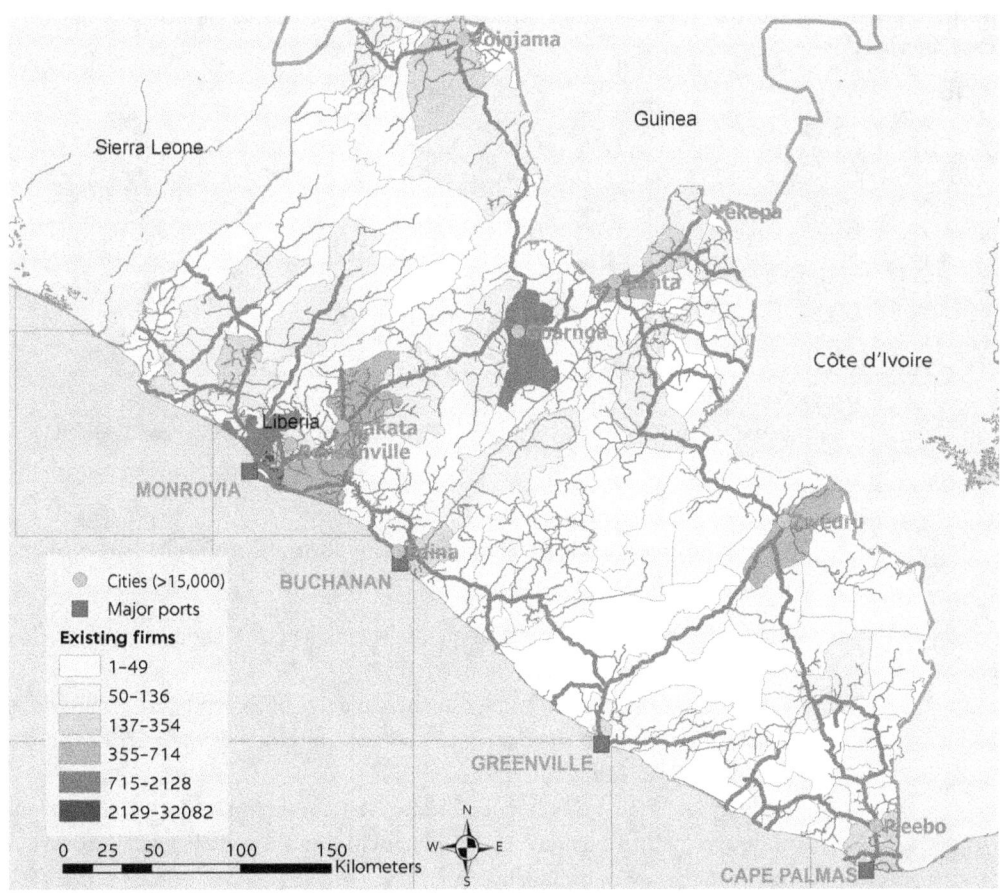

FIGURE ES.6
The firm distribution is more skewed than the population distribution

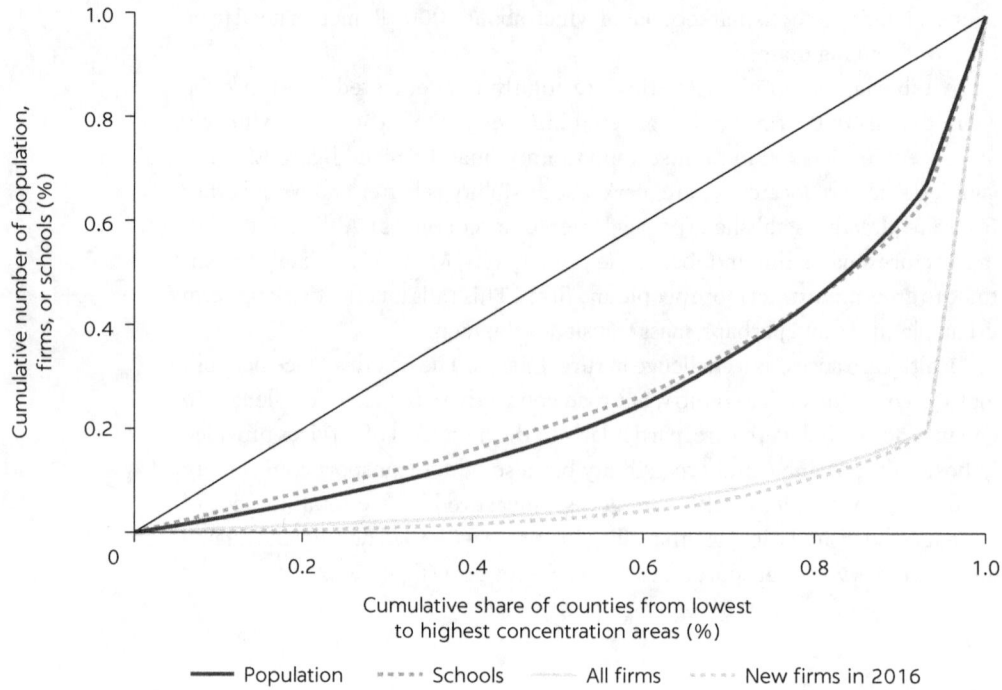

FIGURE ES.7
Better transport infrastructure can help improve people's access to health care services

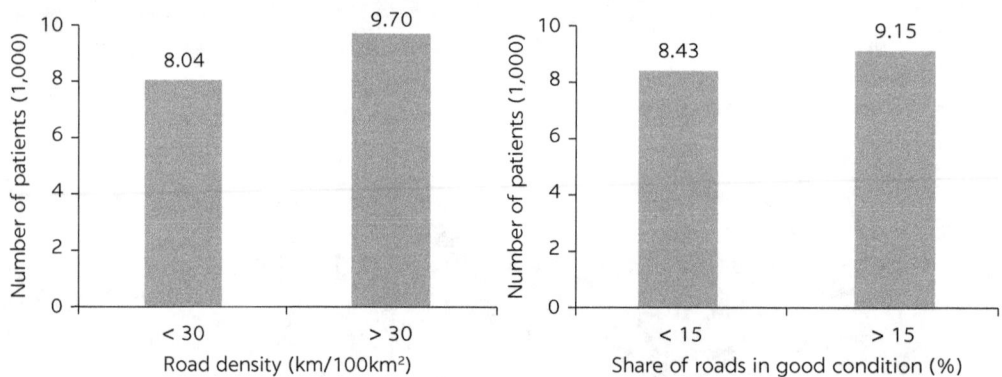

Opportunities and challenges. Liberia's opportunities and challenges can be summarized as follows:

- Road coverage is sufficient, but quality remains poor. Cabotage is one option for improving north-south connectivity
- Port access is generally good, but the capacity of Freeport of Monrovia is constrained. Other ports may have potential, although economies of scale in port operations cannot be ignored
- Railways may be a way to connect the Ganta area to the port of Buchanan, although institutional arrangements, including the existing rail concession agreement, may be a challenge

- Regional trade is limited, although Bong and Nimba Counties are relatively well connected to neighboring countries. Increasing rail line connectivity and improving the inland road network might enhance regional trade activities
- Greater connectivity can stimulate agricultural production. Among others, rural access to the road network and market accessibility are important constraints
- Fisheries have the potential to make seafood a net exporting industry, rather than a net importer. Feeder road connectivity from landing sites to markets needs to be improved
- It is likely that cities, especially Monrovia, will continue to grow because of agglomeration economies. Monrovia is likely to become more congested; intercity linkages need to be strengthened for other cities to have better market access.

Tentative financial resource requirements. Given a wide range of connectivity needs, strategic prioritization is required. Although further detailed assessments will be needed, it is tentatively estimated that the road sector would need at least US$3,433 million to maintain the primary road network and provide universal rural access (table ES.1). Additional resources would be required for road structures and road maintenance as well as other complementary investments, such as ports, railway, and logistics. In this calculation, a simple assumption was made: road rehabilitation costs US$1 million for paved roads and US$75,000 for gravel roads. All classified roads will be rehabilitated if they are not in good condition. Additional roads may be needed to provide universal access in rural areas given the fact that some people live beyond the current official road network (when 2 km access is considered).

If financial requirements to improve connectivity are classified by development objectives, the agricultural sector, including crop and fishery production, would likely require the largest amount of resources, followed by the health sector. Note that the current report does not provide exhaustive assessment. However, US$333 million may be needed to provide better market access to half of Liberia's main crop production areas (table ES.2). Another US$100 million would be needed to connect fishery landing sites. Although many costs are overlapped with agricultural needs, it is estimated that US$330 million would be needed to ensure health care access in the country. Regional connectivity would require at least US$112 million and coastal city connectivity may need US$133 million or more. There are other physical and institutional components that remain to be further assessed for these options. Climate resilience, which also

TABLE ES.1 **Liberia's financial needs estimates by road classification**

OBJECTIVES/INTERVENTIONS	FINANCIAL NEEDS (US$ MILLION)
1. Primary road network	2,230
Rehabilitate paved primary roads	78
Upgrade unpaved primary roads	2,152
2. Universal rural access	1,203
Rehabilitate the current road network	606
Construct (or reclassify) new rural roads	597

TABLE ES.2 **Liberia's financial needs estimates by development objective**

OBJECTIVES/INTERVENTIONS	FINANCIAL NEEDS (US$ MILLION)
A. Promote major agricultural production	333
Connect top 15% major production areas to markets	108
Connect half of crop production areas to markets	225
B. Promote fishery production	101
Connect landing sites to domestic markets	101
C. Improve health access	330
Connect major hospitals to Monrovia	207
Connect district centers to major hospitals	124
D. Improve connectivity among coastal cities	At least 133
Expand the capacity of Freeport of Monrovia	—
Develop cabotage between Monrovia and other ports	—
Improve inland road connectivity from 3 ports (Buchanan, Greenville and Harper)	133
E. Improve rail connectivity between hinterland and Buchanan	—
Introduce non-mining freight operations to Lamco rail line	—
F. Promote regional connectivity by road	At least 112
Rehabilitate main regional corridors	112
Improve border crossing facilities and arrangements	—
G. Strengthen climate resilience	103–1,155
Rehabilitate or upgrade roads that are located in flood-prone areas and in poor condition	103–1,155

Source: World Bank based on data provided by the government of Liberia.
Note: — denotes that the information is unavailable as of publication date.

requires further detailed analysis, is likely to add to the cost of improving sustainability of transport infrastructure.

Who could finance? In theory, taxpayers or road users can finance road infrastructure. Fiscal space of the government of Liberia is limited. Concessionaires are one of the heavy road users in the country. Mining, agriculture, and forestry concessionaires contribute more than US$100 million or 6–10 percent of GDP every year. There is an important opportunity for the government to collaborate with them to share the responsibility for road investment. Nearly 40 percent of the country's land area is currently devoted to extractive concessions. In these concession areas, there are about 3,900 kilometers of roads or one-third of the country's total road network, of which 88 percent are not in good condition.

Liberia has an emerging experience in engaging the private sector for the development of various infrastructure projects, which have contributed to the economic development of the nation. As in 2014, forestry is the largest concession sector in Liberia, followed by agriculture, energy, and mining. The general legal framework for public procurement in Liberia is robust and complies with most of the international best practices considering its relevance to both the Public Expenditure Budgeting and Financial Accountability Performance Measurement Framework (PEFA). The National Bureau of Concessions Act, Public Procurement and Concessions Commission (PPCC) Act, and Extractive

Industries Transparency Initiative (EITI), the legal framework that governs concessions, is also in place.

Concessionaires have dealt with the vulnerability of the transport infrastructure in the country in different ways. Some have directly developed their own port, rail, and energy infrastructure, while others also operate significant portions of the rural road network. Third-party access to concession infrastructure is normally granted as long as spare capacity exists. This is the case for ports and railways. On the other hand, right to public infrastructure, such as public roads, is assured for concessionaires with no obligation to pay for repair or maintenance of such roads, unless they are the sole user. There are cases where additional payment obligations are included that can be used to develop transport infrastructure in local areas. For instance, under the Maryland Oil Palm Plantation concession agreement, the provisions require the concessionaire to contribute US$5 per hectare annually to the community development fund and 1 percent of its annual gross sales of oil palm-related products to the oil palm development fund.

There is an opportunity to develop transport infrastructure in partnership with the private sector in Liberia. However, some policies need to be strengthened. It is imperative to further develop provisions for access and intermodal connectivity with road, rail, and port assets, with the support of the government, to seek optimal utilization of the resources by both the government and the concessionaires. It is imperative that the policies to award concessions with infrastructure provisions to the private developers should be considered in keeping with the National Transportation Policy of Liberia. Systematic application of infrastructure provisions is needed to avoid fragmented transport infrastructure developments and improve the overall regional connectivity.

Future works. Further works are needed to fine-tune the results and complete the prioritization framework, with missing data collected and other institutional issues examined. More discussion is needed to develop an actual prioritization mechanism. A set of criteria and weights need to be agreed on. More importantly, not only physical interventions, but also institutional frameworks and other complementary policies need to be further examined. Currently, the government of Liberia is preparing a national transport master plan for which this report, hopefully, provides a lot of useful insights.

Abbreviations

BMC	Bong Mines Company
CFMA	Community Forest Management Agreement
CQS	consultant's qualification selection
EEA	European Economic Area
EITI	Extractive Industries Transparency Initiative
EOI	expression of interest
FBS	fixed-budget selection
FDA	Forestry Development Authority
FMC	forest management contract
FUP	forest use permit
GDO	Government Diamond Office
GDP	gross domestic product
GI	global integrity
IMCC	Inter-Ministerial Concessions Committee
IMO	International Maritime Organization
ISM	International Safety Management
ISPS	International Ship and Port Facility Security
LCS	least-cost selection
LEITI	Liberia Extractive Industries Transparency Initiative
LMC	Liberia Mining Company
MAI	market access index
MLME	Ministry of Lands, Mines and Energy
MoA	Ministry of Agriculture
MT	metric tons
NBC	National Bureau of Concessions
NIC	National Investment Commission
NIMASA	Nigerian Maritime Administration and Safety Agency
NIOC	National Iron Ore Company
NMA	Nigerian Maritime Authority
NOCAL	National Oil Company of Liberia
NPA	National Port Authority
PEFA	Public Expenditure and Financial Accountability
PPC	Public Procurement and Concessions
PPCC	Public Procurement Concession Commission

PPP	public-private partnership
PSC	production sharing contract
PUP	private use permit
RAI	rural access index
RFP	Request for Proposal
SSS	short sea shipping
TEU	twenty-foot equivalent unit
TSC	timber sale contract

1 Introduction

Prior to the Ebola crisis in 2014, Liberia was experiencing robust economic growth at an average rate of more than 7 percent a year, mainly driven by strong mining activities supported by high international commodity prices (figure 1.1). The Liberian economy has traditionally depended greatly on the export of natural resources, such as iron ore and rubber. From an employment perspective, agriculture is also an important sector, employing approximately half of the labor force, whereas the manufacturing sector is limited,[1] although agricultural productivity is low (figure 1.2). The vast majority of agricultural production is subsistence farming with limited market transactions on the input or output side. Many rural farmers are not well connected to markets and live below the poverty line. The national poverty rate in Liberia is high—estimated at 54.1 percent in 2008 (LISGIS 2009).

Significant challenges lie ahead as the economy recovers from the Ebola crisis. Many development efforts have been suspended in recent years. There remains a risk of rapid spread of infectious disease in Liberia and neighboring countries. The economy is still vulnerable to economic shocks; international commodity prices may continue to fluctuate; fiscal balances are likely to deteriorate in the short term; and overall economic activities will be slow at least for the next couple of years.

To effectively use limited resources, strategic planning and prioritization of public investment is essential and more crucial than ever before. It is important to understand what the unmet infrastructure needs are and what economic opportunities remain unexploited in the country.

The Ebola crisis revealed the vulnerability of the country's transport and health systems to unexpected external shocks. Liberia owns various transport infrastructure assets, including roads and other transport modes such as railways, but transport connectivity does not seem to have been sufficient to address emergencies such as a rapid pandemic, particularly in rural and remote areas.

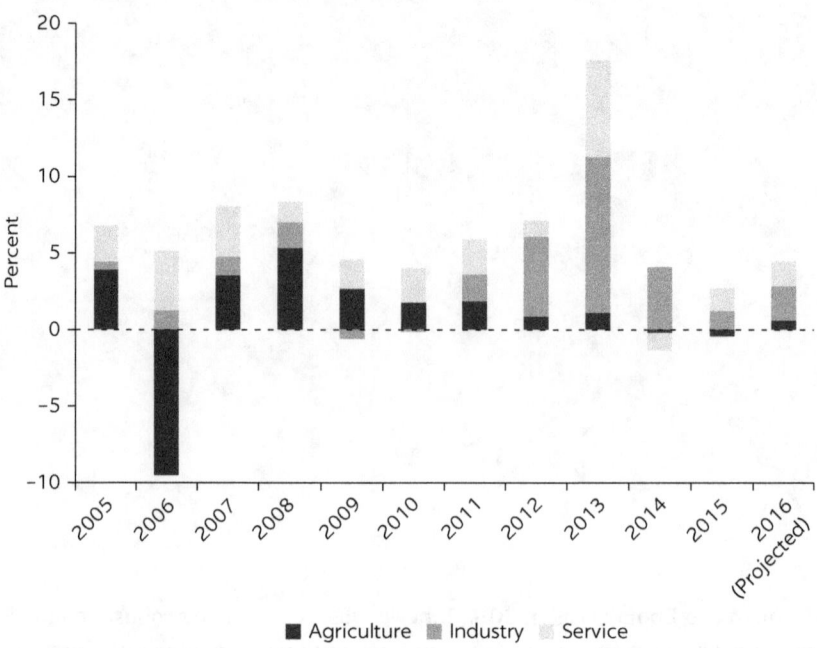

FIGURE 1.1
Liberia: gross domestic product growth rate

Source: World Development Indicators; International Monetary Fund.

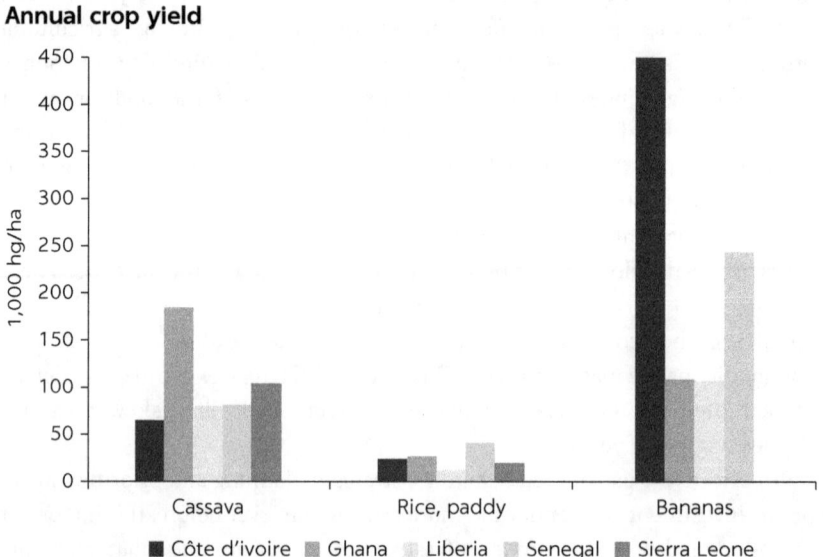

FIGURE 1.2
Annual crop yield

Source: Food and Agriculture Organization Corporate; Statistical Database.

Liberia is an urbanized economy (figure 1.3). Economic activities are highly concentrated in Monrovia, where more than 1.2 million people, or 55 percent of the total urban population, live (map 1.1), although approximately 2.2 million people, or half of the total population, live in rural areas (figure 1.4). It is projected that the rural population will increase to some 2.8 million by 2030 (UN-Habitat 2013). Thus, the lack of rural connectivity remains an important challenge.

FIGURE 1.3
Urbanization rate

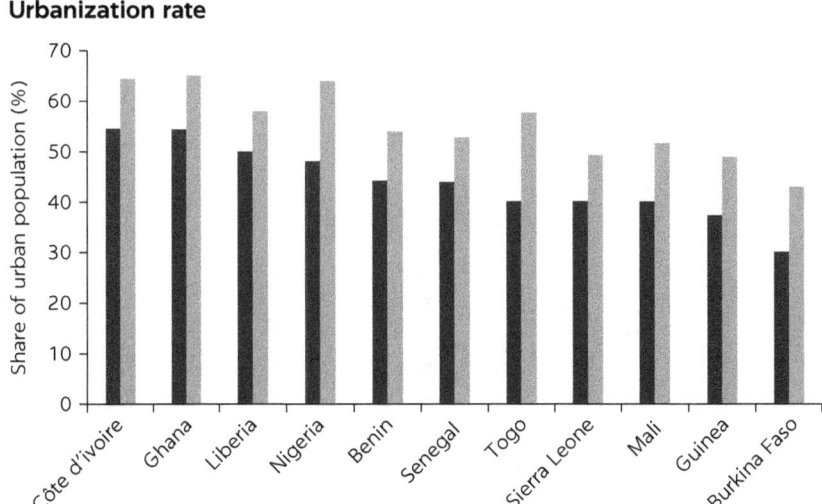

Source: World Development Indicators; United Nations Human Settlements Program.

MAP 1.1
Population distribution and road network

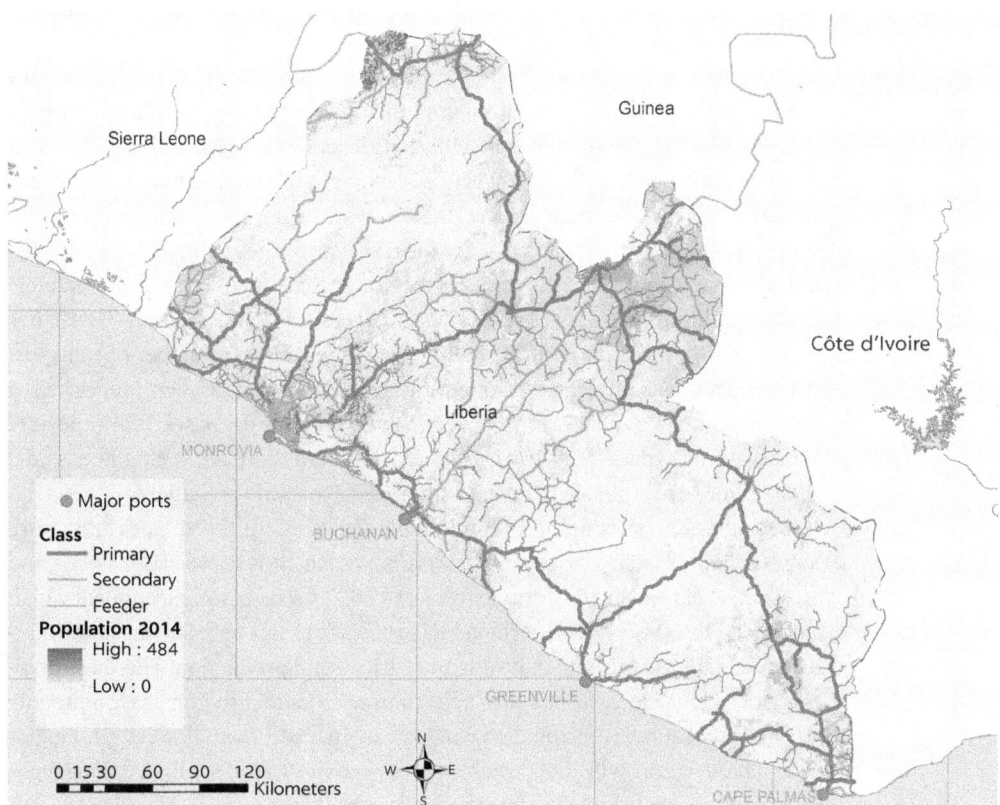

Source: WorldPop; Africa Infrastructure Country Diagnostic.

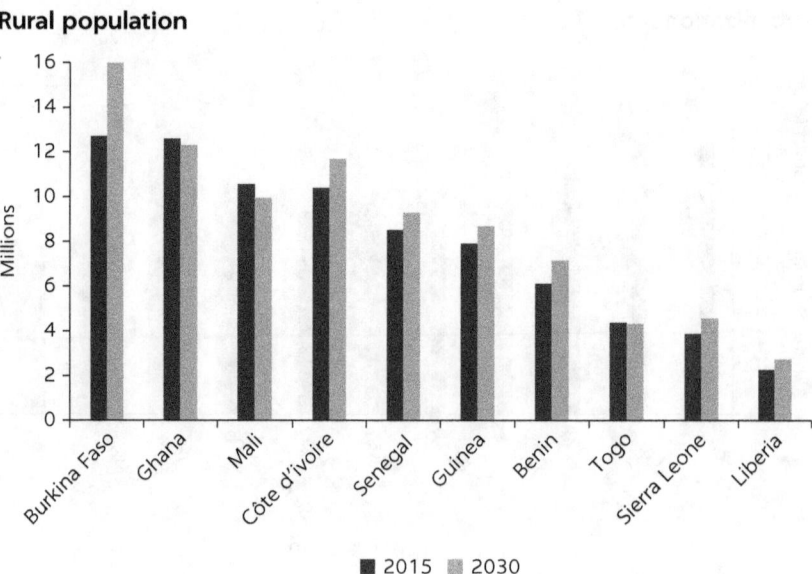

FIGURE 1.4
Rural population

■ 2015 ■ 2030

Source: World Development Indicators; United Nations Human Settlements Program.

The rural population has particularly poor access to social facilities. A recent study showed that people live an average of 7.2 kilometers from the nearest health facility. It takes on average more than two hours to reach the nearest health facility on foot (Kruk et al. 2010).

The available literature generally supports the argument that better transport connectivity stimulates agricultural growth and job creation (Bell and van Dillen 2012), improving access to social facilities such as schools (Khandker, Bakht, and Koolwal 2009) and reducing poverty (Dercon et al. 2007), although in Liberia, there is no solid evidence or analysis that shows how improved transport connectivity could benefit the economy. Since the civil war, the government has dedicated considerable resources to the transport sector. It is estimated that approximately US$160 million, or 7.9 percent of Liberia's gross domestic product (GDP), has been spent on roads and bridges every year (figure 1.5).[2] A number of transport projects have been implemented or are currently under preparation. Some needed to be implemented quickly for recovery and emergency purposes. It is important to understand what effects can be expected, where there are unmet needs, and what options are available to unleash untapped economic potential.

Climate change is an additional challenge, making these questions more complex. It is projected that some natural disasters such as sea level rise, floods, and occasional heat waves will become worse. In 2007, for instance, exceptionally high rainfall led to massive floods, which had implications not only for transport infrastructure, but also for human health and agricultural production. There is significant uncertainty in currently available climate models, although it is commonly projected that annual precipitation will increase in Liberia, as will average temperature.[3] These factors will affect transport connectivity. In the medium to long term, more resilience may be called for when transport infrastructure is developed.

The goals of this report were to consolidate available spatial and subnational data in Liberia, examine Liberia's transport constraints and economic opportunities through a spatial lens, and analyze the possible effect of improved transport connectivity on the economy. Along with other datasets, road condition data were updated using a new smartphone application. The data cover the

FIGURE 1.5
Government expenditures on road development

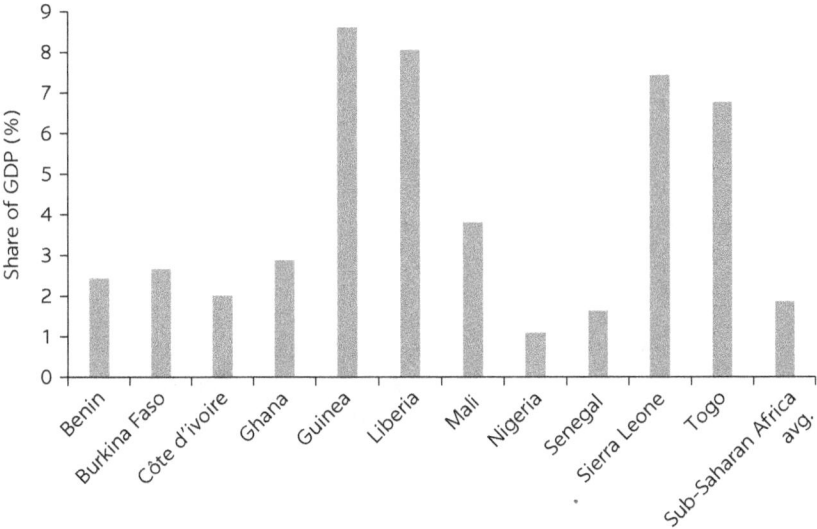

Source: World Bank estimate for Liberia; Africa Infrastructure Country Diagnostic for other countries.

entire road network in Liberia and allow a variety of analyses related to transport connectivity to be conducted.

The remaining chapters of the report are organized as follows: Chapter 2 examines the current transport infrastructure, primarily the road network; Chapter 3 examines domestic connectivity from various aspects; Chapter 4 addresses broader issues, such as regional connectivity and multimodality of the transport system; Chapter 5 provides some evidence of the possible economic effect of transport connectivity. The analyses establish not only correlations between transport infrastructure and economic activities, but also their causality, although the identification strategy, which depends on data availability, may not be strong. Chapter 6 discusses financial requirements. Chapter 7 provides a conclusion.

Limitations of the report. There are important caveats that need to considered in any discussion of this report. First, the data may not be up to date or may lack sufficient granularity. A number of assumptions and approximations were made to address these gaps. The main results are largely robust regardless of the assumptions, although some results may be sensitive to them. Second, the report discusses some of the economic benefits of improved transport connectivity, although it covers only some benefits that materialize on the ground. For instance, transport externalities, such as air pollution and safety, are outside the scope of the report. Finally, related to the above, the report takes a partial equilibrium approach. Each of the individual results is reliable and robust, but the overall results, if all of the effects were combined, were not determined. More dynamic analysis is needed.

NOTES

1. World Development Indicators.
2. According to the Public Expenditure Review conducted in 2013, approximately 70 percent of government capital expenditures are on roads and bridges. Based on the International

Monetary Fund's projection, capital spending would amount to US$230 million in 2017. Liberia's GDP is approximately US$2 billion.
3. See Liberia's risk screening overview based on the World Bank Climate Change Knowledge Portal.

REFERENCES

Bell, Clive, and Susanne van Dillen. 2012. "How Does India's Rural Roads Program Affect the Grassroots? Finding from a Survey in Orissa." World Bank Policy Research Working Paper 6167, World Bank, Washington, DC.

Dercon, Stefan, Daniel O. Gilligan, John Hoddinott, and Tassew Woldehanna. 2007. "The Impact of Roads and Agricultural Extension on Consumption Growth and Poverty in Fifteen Ethiopian Villages." CSAE WPS/2007-01, Oxford University, Oxford, UK.

Khandker, Shahidur R., Zaid Bakht, and B. Gayatri Koolwal. 2009. "The Poverty Impact of Rural Roads: Evidence from Bangladesh." *Economic Development and Cultural Change* 57 (4): 685–722.

Kruk, Margaret E., Peter C. Rockers, Elizabeth H. Williams, S. Tornorlah Varpilah, Rose Macauley, Geetor Saydee, and Sandro Galea. 2010. "Availability of Essential Health Services in Post-Conflict Liberia." *Bulletin of the World Health Organization* 88: 527–34.

LISGIS (Liberia Institute of Statistics and Geo-Information Services). 2009. *Liberia: 2008 National Population and Housing Census Final Results*. Monrovia, Liberia: Liberia Institute of Statistics and Geo-Information Services.

UN-Habitat (United Nations Human Settlements Programme). 2013. *State of the World's Cities: Prosperity of Cities. 2012/2013*.

2 The Current Road Network

ROADS

Liberia's road network is considered sufficient in terms of coverage. It seems to cover every part of the country from a geographic point of view. There are different estimates of total road length because of the lack of georeferenced road network data. According to official statistics, Liberia has approximately 9,916 kilometers of roads, of which 734 kilometers are paved (table 2.1) (Ministry of Transport 2012). This translates into a road density of 10.3 kilometers per 100 km^2 of land, which is not particularly high but is reasonably comparable with that of other small countries in the region (e.g., 8.1 kilometers in Senegal, 11.9 kilometers in Sierra Leone, 12.6 kilometers in Ghana) (figure 2.1). Based on a global population distribution dataset, WorldPop, it is estimated that Liberia's current road network reaches approximately 73 percent of the total population.[1]

Road quality has long been a matter of concern. The road network deteriorated significantly because of the chronic lack of maintenance during and since the long civil war. Considerable resources are needed to restore the road network. The total cost of reestablishing the basic road and bridge network is estimated to be approximately US$1 billion (Ministry of Transport 2012). In recent years, the government of Liberia has made significant efforts toward rehabilitating the main corridors, although the unmet financial needs are still likely to be enormous.

Although the paved road network is relatively well maintained, the condition of unpaved roads is generally poor or very poor. A nationwide road inventory survey was conducted using a smartphone application in May 2016, to update the data on the condition of the road network[2]; 11,423 kilometers of roads were surveyed (map 2.1), which is 15 percent more than the previous road length

TABLE 2.1 **Liberia's road network**
Length (km)

	PAVED	UNPAVED	TOTAL
Primary	734	1,130	1,864
Secondary	0	2,350	2,350
Feeder	0	5,702	5,702
Total	734	9,182	9,916

Source: Ministry of Public Works.

FIGURE 2.1
Road density

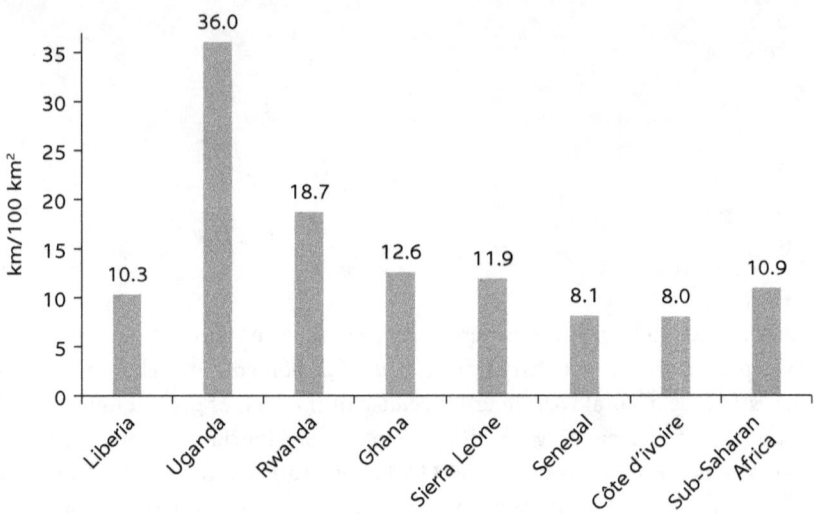

Source: Ministry of Public Works; Africa Infrastructure Country Diagnostic database.

estimate (table 2.2).[3] This is probably the most accurate estimate ever. More than 90 percent of paved roads are in good or fair condition, but nearly 60 percent of unpaved roads are in poor or very poor condition (figure 2.2). In the survey, the road conditions were classified based on measured roughness (international roughness index). An international norm was used for condition classification (table 2.3).

The survey results cover more primary and feeder roads and fewer secondary roads than previous official estimates. The secondary and tertiary road networks, which constitute last-mile connectivity in rural areas, are in particularly poor condition. Unpaved primary roads also need to be improved. Approximately 40 percent of primary roads, 50 percent of secondary roads, and 60 percent of tertiary roads are in poor or very poor condition (table 2.4). These figures compare less favorably with Liberia's neighbors. For instance, 48 percent of tertiary roads in Sierra Leone and 41 percent in Côte d'Ivoire are in poor condition. The average in sub-Saharan Africa is 43 percent (figure 2.3).

The first priority should be maintenance of the good condition of the road network. Three main corridors (Monrovia to Ganta; Buchanan, Liberia's second-largest port; and Bo Waterside, a border crossing point with Sierra Leone) are in good condition. These are all paved roads and should be maintained in good condition. Unpaved roads also need to be improved and maintained.

MAP 2.1
Liberia's road network condition, 2016

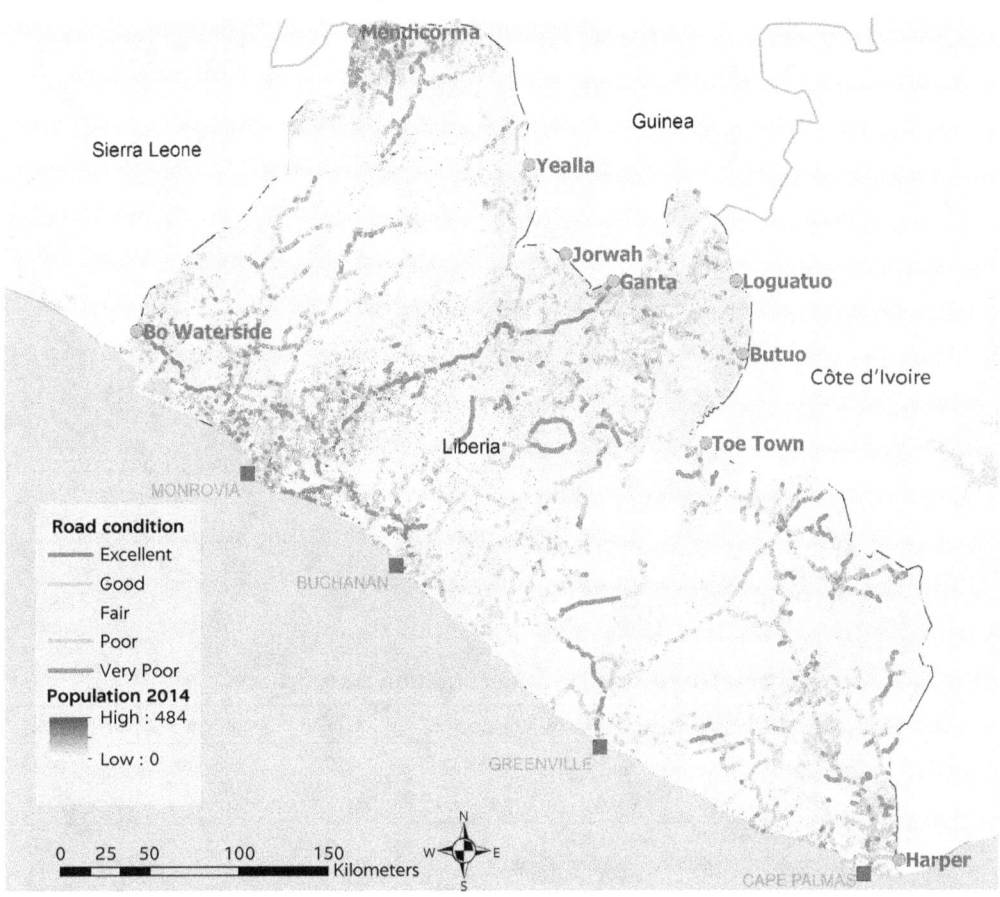

Source: World Bank survey.

TABLE 2.2 **Results of road inventory survey according to surface type**
Length (km)

	TOTAL	ROAD CONDITION				
		EXCELLENT	GOOD	FAIR	POOR	VERY POOR
Paved	565	398	89	42	20	16
Unpaved	10,857	216	409	3,996	4,745	1,491
Total	11,423	615	498	4,038	4,765	1,507

Source: World Bank survey.

Most are currently in poor condition, with conditions generally worse in more remote and inland areas. Sustained rural road maintenance is a challenge. Fragmented interventions are unlikely to have a positive impact. Therefore, systematic prioritization and planning are needed.

BRIDGES AND CULVERTS

Road-related structures are crucial for ensuring transport connectivity where the climate is tropical and humid. A significant number of bridges and culverts

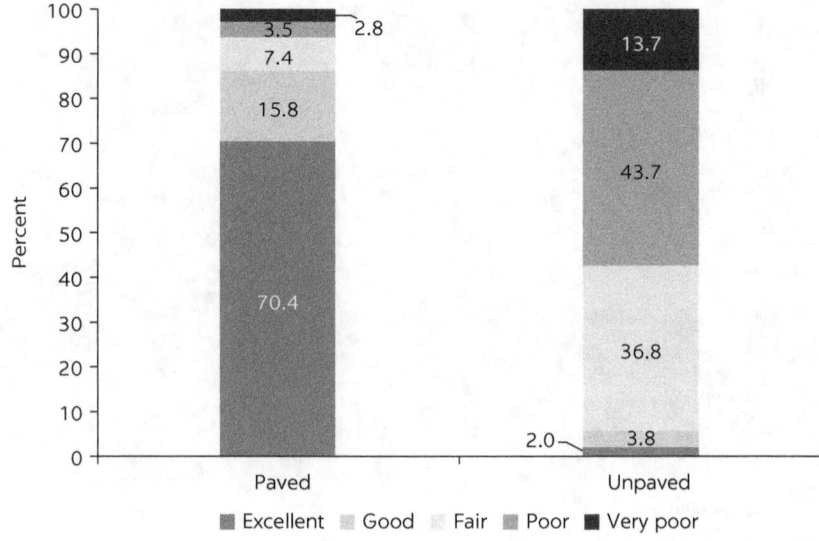

FIGURE 2.2
Liberia's road condition according to surface type

Source: World Bank survey.

TABLE 2.3 **Thresholds for road condition classification**

	EXCELLENT	GOOD	FAIR	POOR	VERY POOR
Paved	<2.5	2.5–4.0	4.0–5.5	5.5–7.0	>7.0
Unpaved	<4.0	4.0–5.0	5.0–9.0	9.0–16.0	>16.0

Source: World Bank survey.
Note: Per International Roughness Index.

TABLE 2.4 **Result of road inventory survey according to road class**
Length (km)

	TOTAL	SURFACE TYPE		ROAD CONDITION				
		PAVED	UNPAVED	EXCELLENT	GOOD	FAIR	POOR	VERY POOR
Primary	1,629	565	2,281	440	176	1,013	1,014	203
Secondary	953	0	1,960	77	102	775	793	214
Feeder	6,616	0	6,616	98	220	2,251	2,958	1,090
Total	11,423	565	10,857	615	498	4,038	4,765	1,507

Source: World Bank survey.

support the Liberian road network. For every 5 kilometers of road, there are on average one bridge and three culverts. More than half of these road structures are currently in poor or very poor condition. Particular attention needs to be paid to bridges; only 15 percent of bridges and 50 percent of culverts are in excellent or good condition.

The condition of bridges and culverts was also examined in the road inventory survey. Along the road network surveyed, 2,884 bridges and 7,651 culverts were surveyed. Approximately half of the bridges were found to be in poor or very poor condition, with the condition unknown for 23 percent (figure 2.4). Rehabilitation work is needed on most of the bridges, except for those along the major corridors (map 2.2).

FIGURE 2.3
Percentage of roads in poor condition

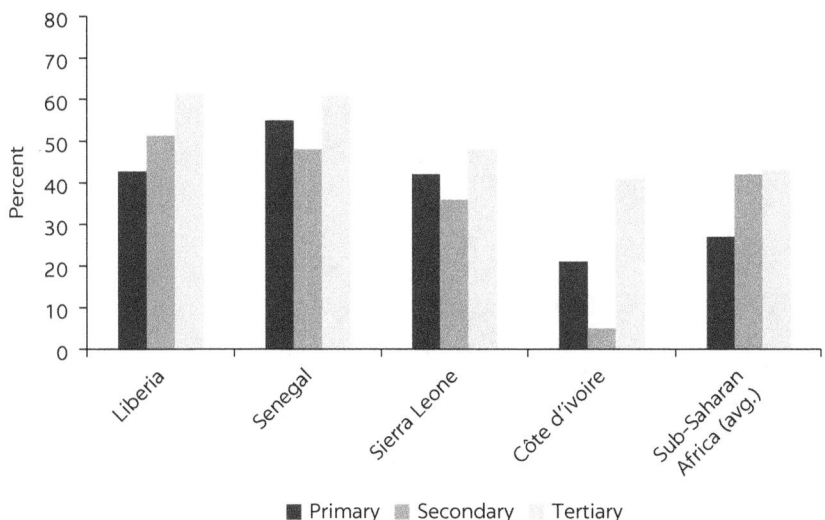

Source: World Bank survey; Africa Infrastructure Country Diagnostic.

FIGURE 2.4
Condition of bridges and culverts

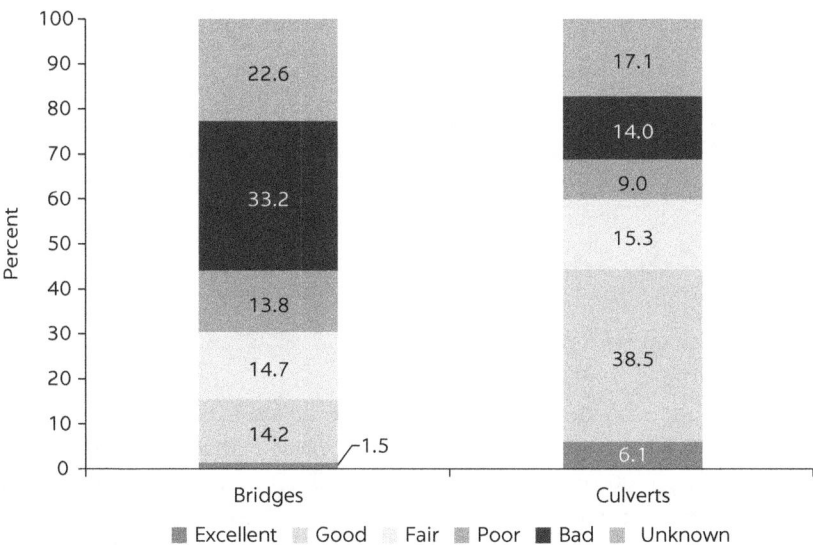

Source: World Bank survey.

Culverts are in better condition, especially along the Monrovia-Ganta corridor, although a significant number of culverts need to be repaired all over the country (map 2.3). The culvert dataset is incomplete because it does not cover areas where culverts are needed but do not currently exist. Further investigation is necessary to assess the potential need for road structures. Given limited resources, improving the condition of the whole network, including road structures, which can be expensive, is a long-term challenge. At the same time, the currently well-maintained paved road network needs to be maintained in good condition.

MAP 2.2
Bridges: location and condition

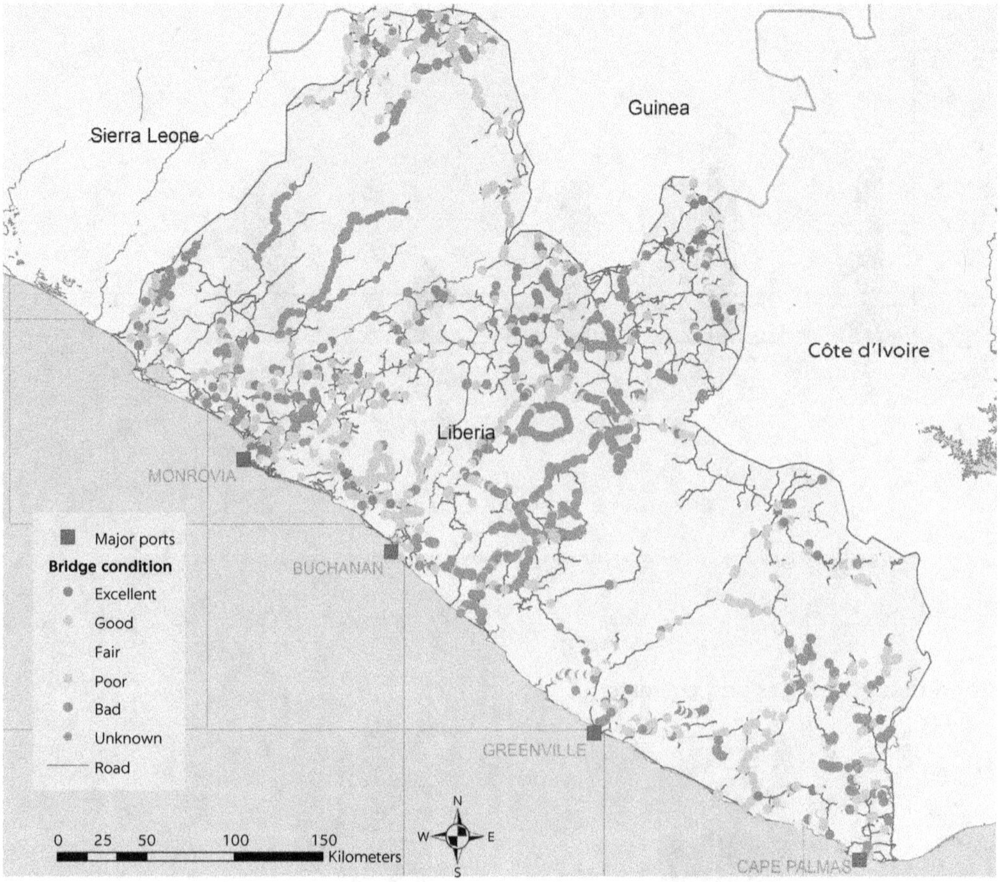

Source: World Bank survey.

CLIMATE VULNERABILITY

Liberia is vulnerable to climate events such as floods, sea level rise, and heat waves. In 2007, exceptionally high rainfall caused floods in West Africa. Approximately 17,000 people were affected in Liberia (Samimi, Fink, and Paeth 2012). A significant amount of water and transport infrastructure was damaged. The currently available climate models indicate that Liberia may be likely to have more floods in the future, but do not predict precisely whether and where more or fewer floods are likely to happen. There is significant variation in projected precipitation.[4]

Regardless of climate change, the current transport infrastructure is already exposed to significant climate risks. For example, floods and downpours can easily wash away unpaved roads that are not properly maintained. According to the road survey, approximately 1,356 kilometers of roads, or approximately 12 percent of the total network, are in flood-prone areas (table 2.5). A 25-year flood map from the Global Assessment Report on Disaster Risk Reduction is used, which is developed by the United Nations International Strategy for Disaster Reduction (map 2.4).

MAP 2.3
Culverts: location and condition

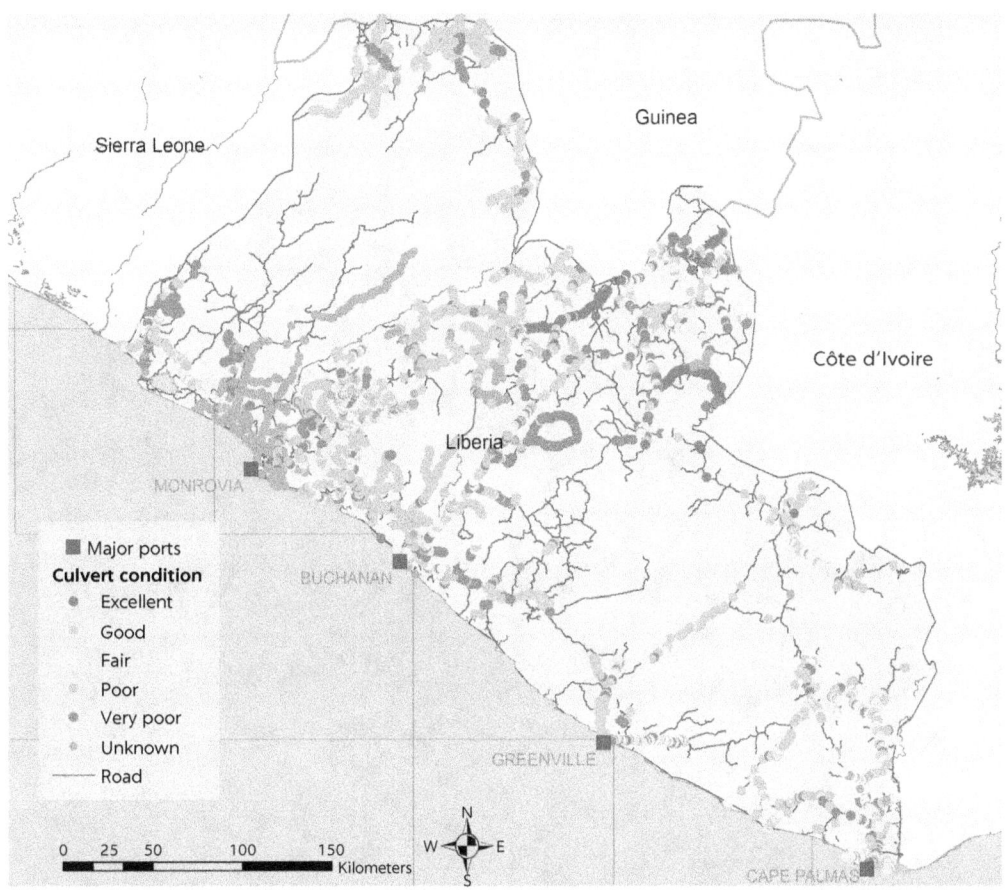

Source: World Bank survey.

TABLE 2.5 **Roads in flood areas**

	FLOOD AREAS		OF WHICH, NOT IN GOOD CONDITION	
	LENGTH (KM)	SHARE (%)	LENGTH (KM)	SHARE (%)
Paved	125	22.0	17	3.0
Unpaved	1,231	11.3	1,138	10.5
Total	1,356	11.9	1,155	10.1

Source: World Bank survey.

Approximately 22 percent of paved roads and 11 percent of unpaved roads are in flood-prone areas, although the paved roads are well maintained and are considered to be resilient to severe climate events. Only 3 percent of paved roads are in poor condition and are located in flood areas.

More unpaved roads in flood-prone areas are in poorer condition than paved roads. Greater attention needs to be paid to this because unpaved roads are generally vulnerable to heavy precipitation because of their engineering characteristics. Approximately 10.5 percent of unpaved roads are in flood-prone areas.

MAP 2.4
Flood-prone areas and road network

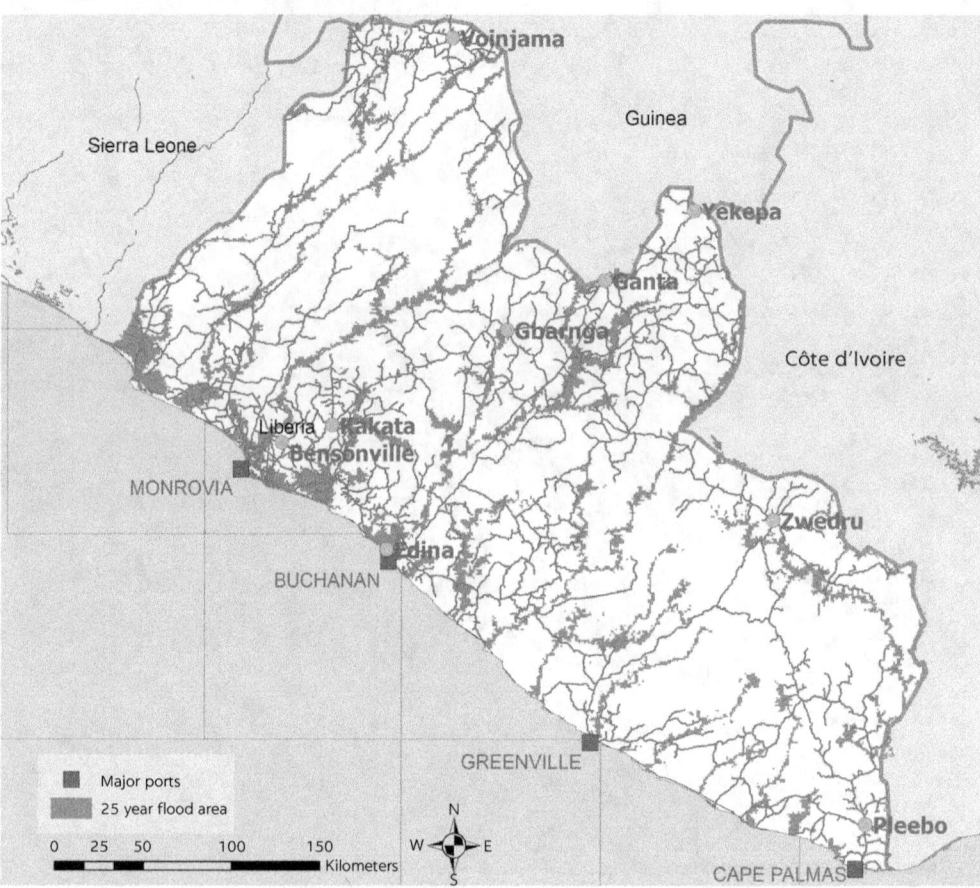

Source: United Nations International Strategy for Disaster Reduction Global Assessment Report database.

TABLE 2.6 **Bridges and culverts in flood-prone areas**

	FLOOD AREA		OF WHICH NOT IN GOOD CONDITION[a]	
	NO.	SHARE (%)	NO.	SHARE (%)
Bridges	244	8.5	181	6.3
Culverts	735	9.6	485	6.3
Roads (km)	1,356	11.9	1,155	10.1

Source: World Bank based on data provided by the government of Liberia.
a. Including structures whose condition is unknown.

Bridges and culverts are critical to mitigating flood risks and ensuring passability even in the rainy season. Contrary to expectations, a small proportion of structures is located in flood-prone areas (table 2.6). According to the road inventory survey, 244 bridges and 735 culverts are located in flood-prone areas, accounting for approximately 9 percent of structures surveyed (12 percent of the road network, 8.5 percent of bridges, 9.6 percent of culverts). More than two-thirds of these structures are in poor condition, indicating weaknesses of Liberia's road network. Rehabilitation and maintenance of these structures will be an important challenge.

NOTES

1. This is estimated by overlaying the WorldPop data and the georeferenced road network data.
2. There are several smartphone applications that allow road roughness to be estimated based on kinematic and GPS sensors in smartphones. For instance, RoadLab is a freely available application. The inventory survey in Liberia used another commercial android application, RoadBump.
3. Urban roads were excluded from the survey.
4. See, for instance, the country dashboard in the World Bank Climate Change Knowledge Portal.

REFERENCES

Ministry of Transport. 2012. "National Transport Master Plan." Ministry of Transport, Monrovia, Liberia.

Samimi, C., A. H. Fink, and H. Paeth. 2012. "The 2007 Flood in the Sahel: Causes, Characteristics and Its Presentation in the Media and FEWS NET." *Natural Hazards and Earth System Sciences* 12: 313–25.

3 Domestic Connectivity

RURAL ACCESSIBILITY

The poor road network has long been a crucial constraint on mobility in Liberia, particularly in rural and remote areas. A new method using spatial data and technique has been developed to measure the Rural Access Index (RAI), which indicates the proportion of people with access to an all-season road within approximately 2 kilometers' walking distance (World Bank 2016a).

The RAI was estimated at 41.9 percent in 2016 in Liberia (map 3.1), which means that approximately 1.6 million rural people had access to a road network in good condition, leaving approximately 2.3 million people unconnected to the road network. The estimated RAI is lower than the initial estimate in 2006, which was 66 percent. Although the two figures cannot be compared directly because the methodologies are different (World Bank 2016a), all indications are that many people in rural areas do not have access to the road network.

Rural accessibility differs substantially between counties and districts. The RAI is high around Monrovia and along the Monrovia-Ganta corridor. Technically, urban areas are excluded from the RAI calculation. Still, the district of Greater Monrovia has a high index of 94.6 percent. Around Monrovia, many districts in Montserrado, Bong, and Nimba Counties also have relatively high RAIs of more than 30 percent. In other districts, RAI is less than 10 percent. For some districts, the RAI is zero, meaning that there is no road in good condition in the district.

It is estimated that recent major road improvement projects helped increase the RAI by 8.4 percent. In recent years, two major road improvement projects were implemented along the Monrovia-Ganta corridor and the Monrovia-Buchanan corridor (map 3.2).[1] These are not rural road projects, but they pass through rural areas. Many rural people along the corridors directly benefited from the improved connectivity. Assuming that the road conditions were poor before the projects, it is estimated that 400,000 people benefited from the projects based on the RAI definition, of whom approximately 328,000 are rural residents (table 3.1).

MAP 3.1
Rural access index, 2016

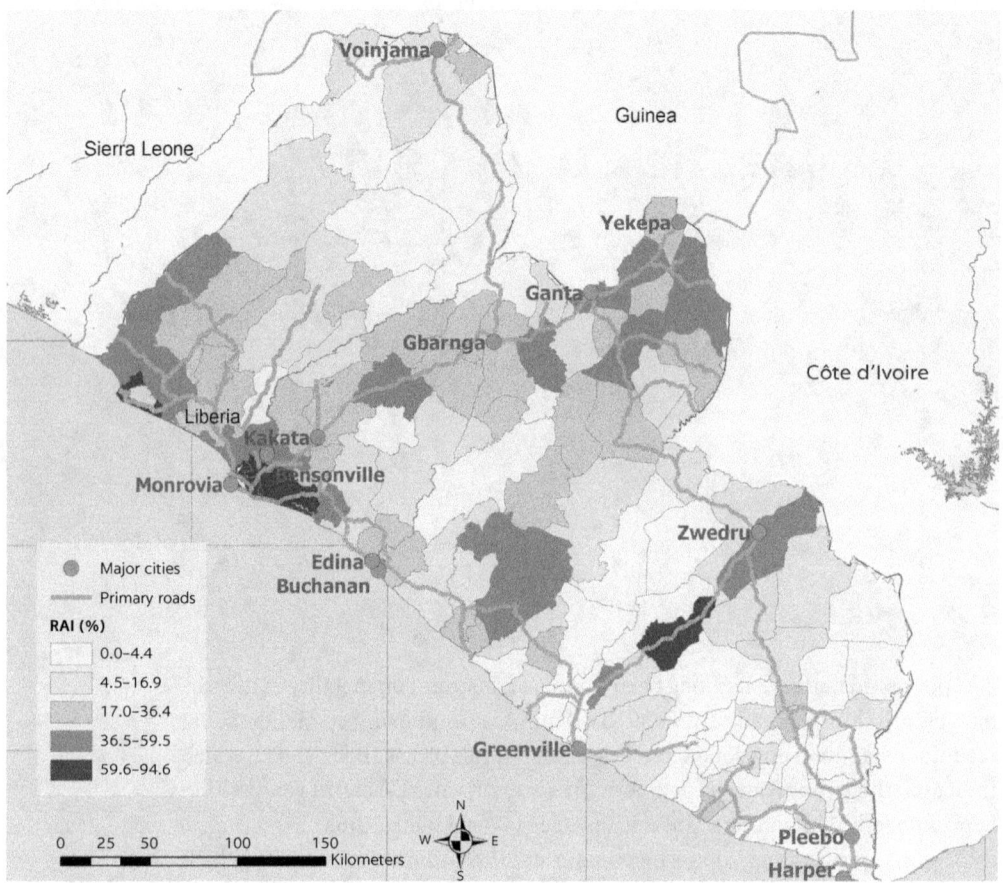

Source: World Bank estimate.

Poverty is persistently high where rural accessibility is low. According to the Household Income and Expenditure Survey (HIES) 2016, the national absolute poverty rate[2] declined from 54.1 percent in 2014 to (LISGIS 2017). While urban poverty declined from 43 percent to 32 percent, rural poverty slightly increased from 70 percent to 72 percent (figure 3.1). Monrovia has a low poverty rate of 20.3 percent, but poverty is more prevalent in inland areas, especially in southern regions (map 3.3). Since the survey methods, such as survey duration, are different between the 2014 and 2016 HIES, it is difficult to compare the two poverty figures.[3] However, a simple comparison at the regional level indicates that poverty declined in Monrovia and the northern areas for the last 2 years. This is broadly consistent with where the major road interventions were carried out, that is, Monrovia-Ganta corridor (figure 3.2). Unsurprisingly, there is broad correlation between poverty incidence and rural accessibility: poverty is high where accessibility is limited (map 3.4). Causality remains open to debate, but rural accessibility seems to be necessary to reduce poverty.

The Sustainable Development Goals were developed to attain universal rural access. Goal 9 is to build a resilient infrastructure, promote inclusive and sustainable industrialization, and foster innovation. Target 9.1 is specifically focused on developing "quality, reliable, sustainable and resilient infrastructure … to support economic development and human well-being, with a focus on affordable and

MAP 3.2
Recent major World Bank–financed road improvement projects

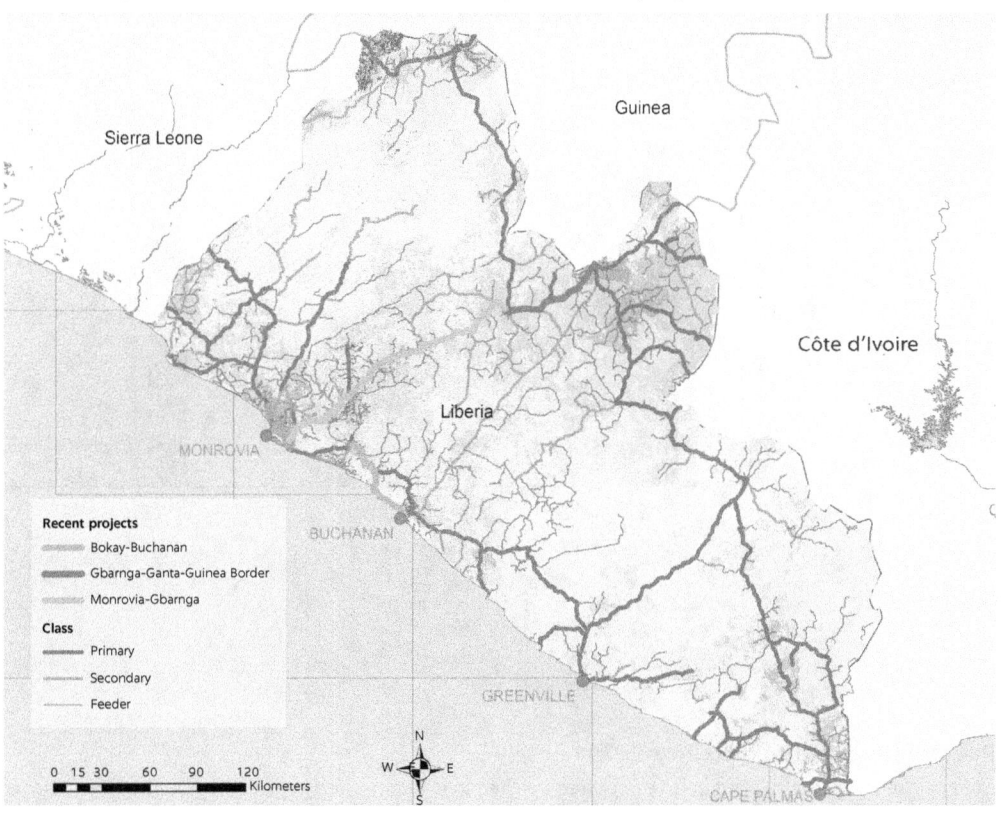

Source: World Bank survey.

TABLE 3.1 **Estimated direct beneficiaries**

	LENGTH (KM)	NUMBER OF BENEFICIARIES[a]		
		URBAN	RURAL	TOTAL
Monrovia-Ganta corridor				
Monrovia-Gbarnga	180	30,293	275,962	306,254
Gbarnga-Ganta-Guinea border	69	10,561	31,221	41,783
Monrovia-Buchanan corridor				
Bokay-Buchanan	56	31,625	21,028	52,653
Total	305	72,479	328,211	400,690

Source: World Bank estimate.
a. Defined according to population living within 2 km of a road.

equitable access for all," for which the RAI is adopted as a core indicator. The RAI developed by Roberts et al. (2006) is one of the few global development indicators in the transport sector. In the initial study based on household surveys, the global RAI was estimated at 68.3 percent, with approximately one billion rural residents without access in 2006. The new method takes advantage of more granular data and consistent methodology based on spatial data and techniques that have recently been developed (World Bank 2016).

The Sustainable Development Goal target is universal access, which is an ambitious goal for Liberia. In recent years, the government of Liberia has

20 | SPATIAL ANALYSIS OF LIBERIA'S TRANSPORT CONNECTIVITY AND POTENTIAL GROWTH

FIGURE 3.1
Absolute poverty rate

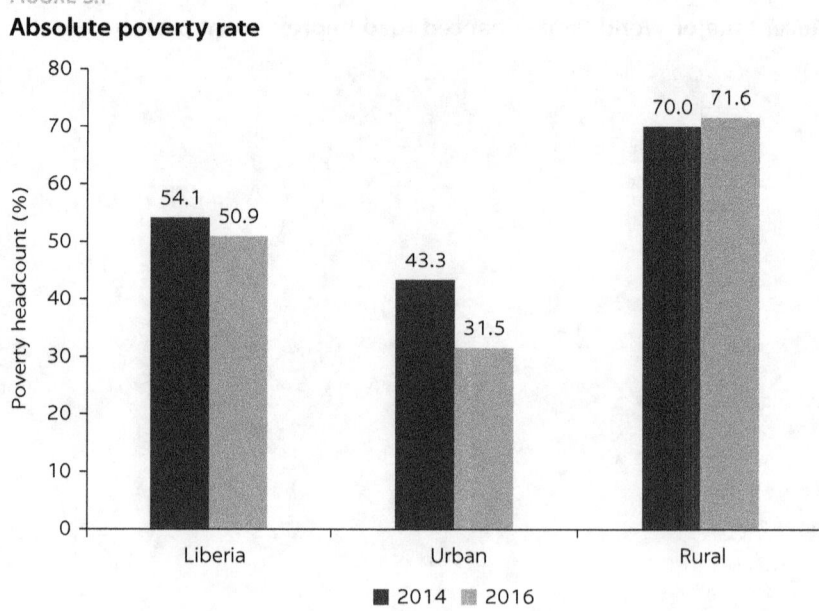

Source: LISGIS 2017.

MAP 3.3
Poverty headcount by county, 2016

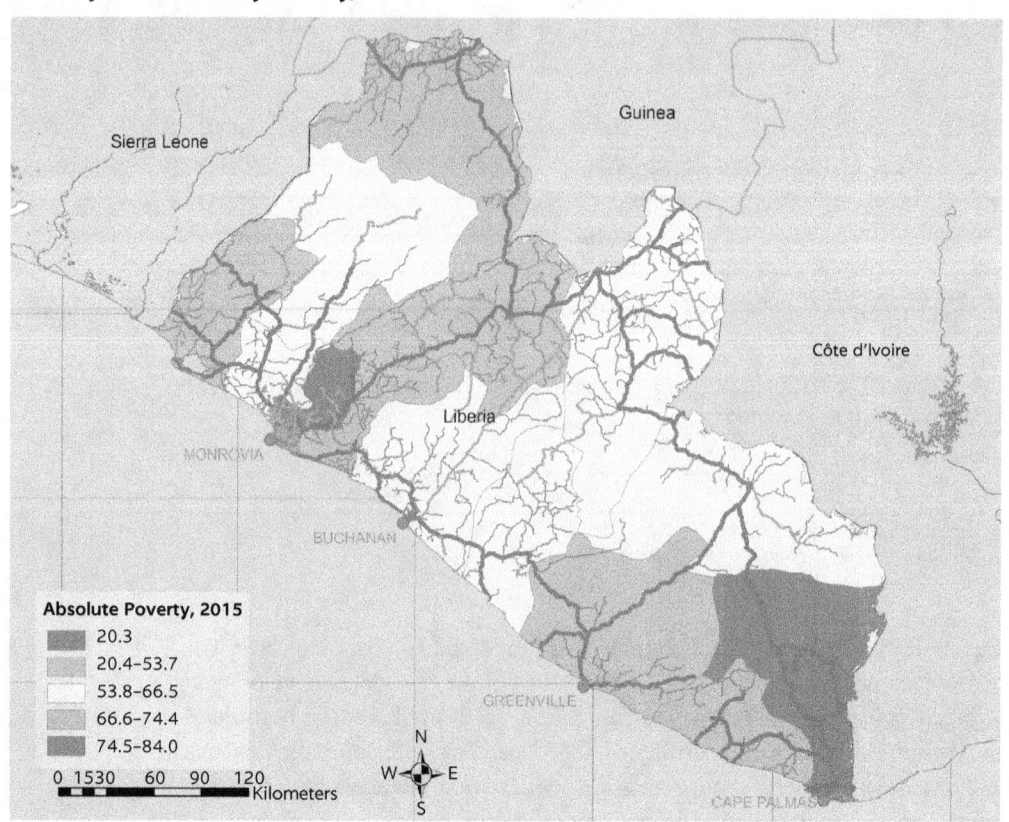

Source: LISGIS 2017.

FIGURE 3.2

Poverty and rural accessibility

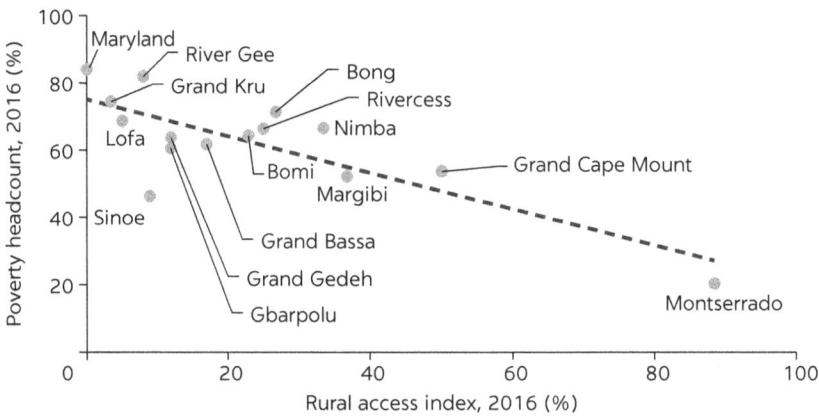

Source: LISGIS 2017; World Bank estimate.

MAP 3.4

Change in poverty rate between 2014 and 2016

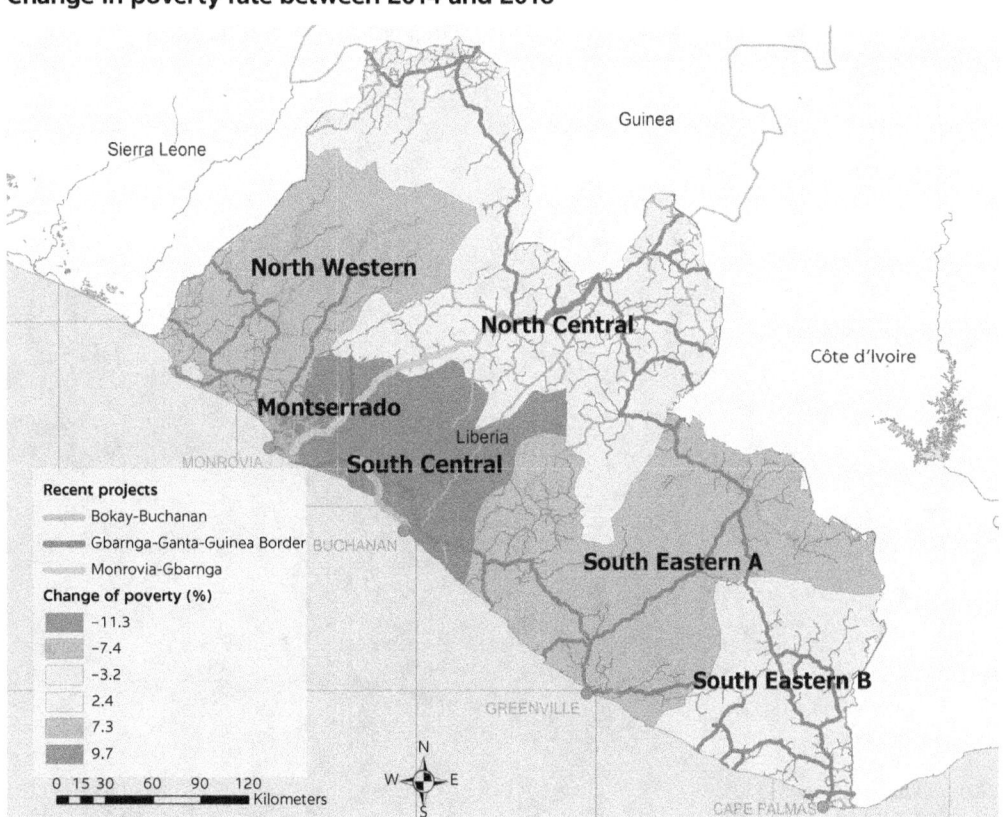

Source: LISGIS 2017; World Bank estimate.

dedicated significant resources to the transport sector. It is estimated that approximately US$160 million, or 7.9 percent of gross domestic product (GDP), is spent on roads and bridges every year.[4] Still, significant additional resources are needed to achieve universal access in rural areas. As a simple back-of-the-envelope calculation, for instance, it is estimated that approximately US$850 million, or 42 percent of GDP, is needed for road rehabilitation works alone.[5] Additional costs would be incurred for maintenance. In addition, as discussed above, many bridges and culverts are in poor condition and need to be repaired. To achieve universal access, some new roads may need to be constructed or reclassified from currently unclassified roads, which would require additional financial resources. The current road network supports only approximately 73 percent of the total rural population, so strategic prioritization is critical.

MARKET ACCESSIBILITY

Although rural accessibility (access to the road network) is the most fundamental connectivity, it is insufficient to support people's diverse needs for mobility. For instance, people need to be connected to markets to take advantage of economic opportunities and social facilities, such as hospitals, to meet their needs. Transport costs to bring one unit of goods to a major market are shown in map 3.5 based on georeferenced road network and condition data. Large cities and towns with more than 15,000 people are used as a proxy of market.

Market accessibility in Liberia is relatively good at the national level. It is estimated that half of the total population lives less than 30 minutes by vehicle from a large city or market (table 3.2) and that 90 percent lives less than 2 hours from

MAP 3.5

Transport costs to market

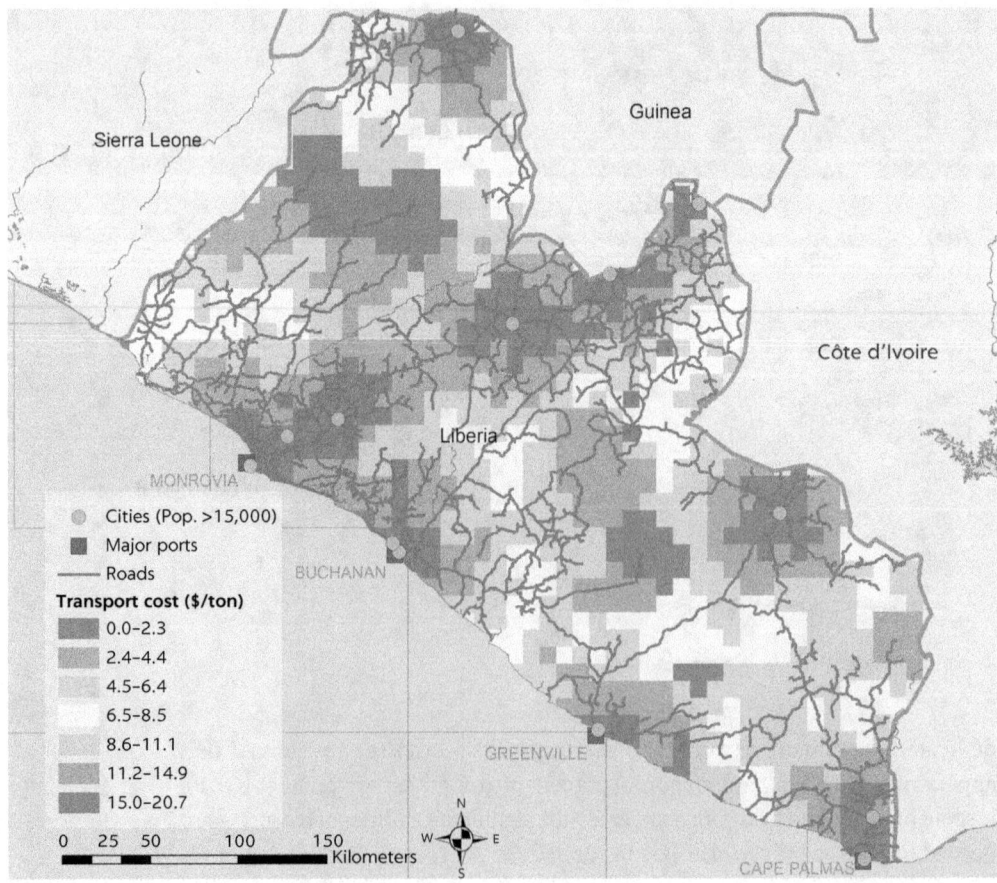

Source: World Bank estimate.

TABLE 3.2 **Population with access to markets**

TRAVEL TIME	POPULATION (1,000)	% OF TOTAL POPULATION
Less than 30 minutes	2,245	52.0
30 minutes–1 hour	755	17.5
1–2 hours	879	20.3
2–4 hours	418	9.7

Source: World Bank estimate.

a large city. The high market accessibility is mainly attributed to Liberia's high urbanization rate. Approximately half of the population lives in urban areas, of which 55 percent are concentrated around the capital city, Monrovia.

Beyond the Monrovia area, market accessibility is also good along the Monrovia-Ganta corridor, where a large number of people live and where transport costs are low because of recent rehabilitation work along the corridor.

Market accessibility is a challenge in other parts of the country, particularly in the north, such as in Gbarpolu County, and the center, such as River Cess and Nimba Counties. Beyond the Monrovia-Ganta corridor, it is estimated that transport costs are high (more than US$10 per ton). It is difficult for people in these areas to take advantage of market opportunities for their livelihoods.

There is a problem of endogeneity between accessibility and population distribution; population density is generally high where transport costs are low. At the same time, transport costs tend to be low where many people live because more road investments are made where more people live.

More formally, market accessibility can be defined according to market capacity with transport and any other constraints taken into account. The simplest formula for market access index (MAI) is based on a conventional gravity model framework, which calculates a sum of purchasing power or market capacity, Y, inversely weighted by the degree of impediment between two locations (e.g., distance, d).[6]

$$MAI_i = \left(\sum_j Y_j / d_{ij}\right) / \max_i (MAI_i)$$

For Y, the city population is used as a proxy for market capacity; d is measured according to transport costs from location i and city j.

On this basis, market accessibility is in even more stark contrast in Liberia because Monrovia's market is much larger than that of other cities. Monrovia has a population of 1.2 million, or one-fourth of Liberia's total population. As the result, market accessibility depends heavily on proximity to Monrovia. Market accessibility is high around Monrovia (map 3.6). The MAI is also relatively high along two well-maintained corridors: Monrovia-Ganta corridor and Monrovia-Bo Waterside road. As a result of these roads, Bong, Bomi, and Grand Cape Mount Counties are considered to be well integrated into the market of Monrovia.

By contrast, the northern and southeastern regions of the country are completely disconnected from the market of Monrovia. In these areas, the road distance from Monrovia is long and road conditions generally poor. There is no significant domestic market in neighboring areas, so the MAI tends to be low.

MAP 3.6
Market access index

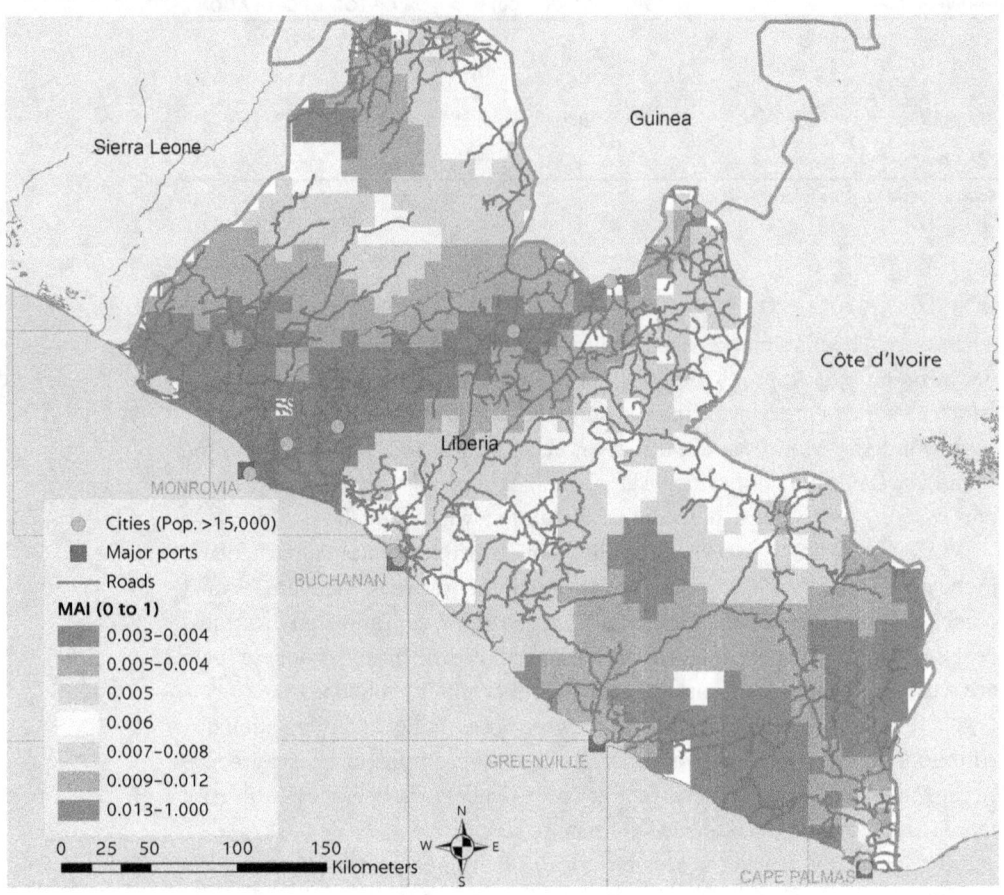

Source: World Bank estimate.

ACCESS TO A PORT

In general, good access to a port is essential to ensure efficient movement of goods, firm productivity, and investment. Available literature suggests that a variety of better transport infrastructure can improve firm productivity and attract investment, fostering agglomeration economies (e.g., Limão and Venables 2001; Holl 2004; Procher 2010).

Seaports are important assets for Liberia. Given poor regional inland connectivity in the country, seaports provide significant access to global and regional markets. Liberia has four major seaports: Freeport of Monrovia, Buchanan, Greenville, and Harper. Historically, these ports have played different roles. Most imports come through Freeport of Monrovia. Iron ore accounts for approximately 35 percent of total throughput at Freeport of Monrovia, followed by clinker (export) and petro products (import). Significant amounts of crops and food products are also imported through Freeport of Monrovia (figure 3.3).

The port of Buchanan is more focused on exporting iron ore, which is produced in northern Nimba County. The Lamco rail line, operated by ArcelorMittal, connects Buchanan to major iron ore sources. Approximately 95 percent of total cargo passing through Buchanan is iron ore. Port operations at Greenville and Harper are much more limited.

FIGURE 3.3

Types of commodities passing through freeport of Monrovia, 2014

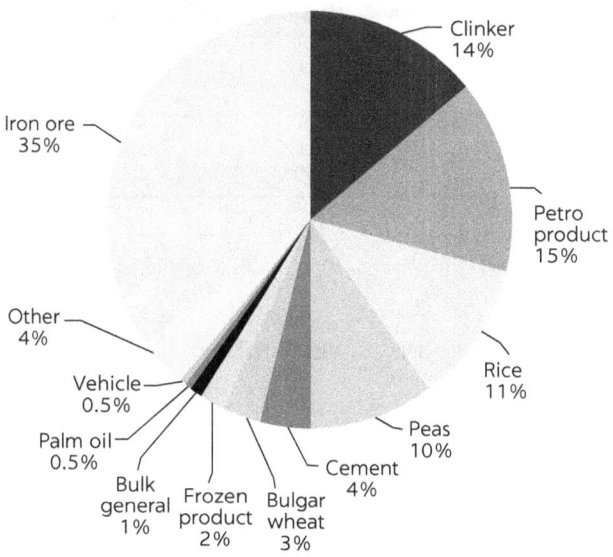

Source: National Port Authority.

TABLE 3.3 **Port traffic in Liberia**

	DEAD WEIGHT (MILLION TONS)		THROUGHPUT (MILLION TONS)				CONTAINER TRAFFIC (TEU)	
			EXPORTS		IMPORTS			
	2013	2014	2013	2014	2013	2014	2013	2014
Freeport of Monrovia	2.683	7.647	0.241	0.971	1.775	1.987	80,448	77,578
Buchanan	3.283	9.823	5.128	5.172	0.004	0.049	139	3,152
Greenville	0.050	0.138	0.032	0.019	0.018	0.004	186	289
Harper	0.026	0.066	0.003	0.004	0.009	0.008	1,309	1,190
Total	6.042	17.674	5.404	6.165	1.807	2.048	82,082	82,209

Source: National Port Authority.
Note: TEU = twenty-foot equivalent units.

According to recent port traffic data, Freeport of Monrovia handles the vast majority of Liberia's import and export traffic. Approximately 98 percent of container traffic passed through Freeport of Monrovia in 2013 (table 3.3), falling slightly to 95 percent in 2014. Import throughputs also declined from 98 percent to 97 percent, possibly because some of the traffic shifted from Freeport of Monrovia to Buchanan, for which the rehabilitation of the Monrovia-(Bokay)-Buchanan corridor in 2014, as discussed above, partly improved road connectivity. Still, port traffic depends heavily on Freeport of Monrovia despite the fact that Buchanan may have the capacity to handle more, although detailed technical data need to be confirmed (table 3.4).

Port operations achieve economies of scale (Wilmsmeier et al. 2006; UNCTAD 2015; World Bank 2016), so larger ports are more efficient, resulting in lower unit costs. Doubling port efficiency could have the same effect as halving the distance between ports (Wilmsmeier et al. 2006). Therefore, it should not be surprising that Liberia relies heavily on Freeport of Monrovia. The country's market size is relatively small, and all neighboring countries have their own ports, except for

TABLE 3.4 **Port infrastructure**

PORT	QUAY LENGTH (M)	DRAFT (M)	YARD AREA (HA)	ANNUAL CAPACITY (1,000 TEU)
Freeport of Monrovia	600	7.5–11	13	75
Buchanan	559	10.5–11.5	—	—
Greenville	400	8.1	—	—
Harper	150	5.5	—	—

Source: National Port Authority.
Note: — denotes that the information is unavailable as of publication date; TEU = twenty-foot equivalent unit.

FIGURE 3.4
Port traffic of selected ports in West Africa

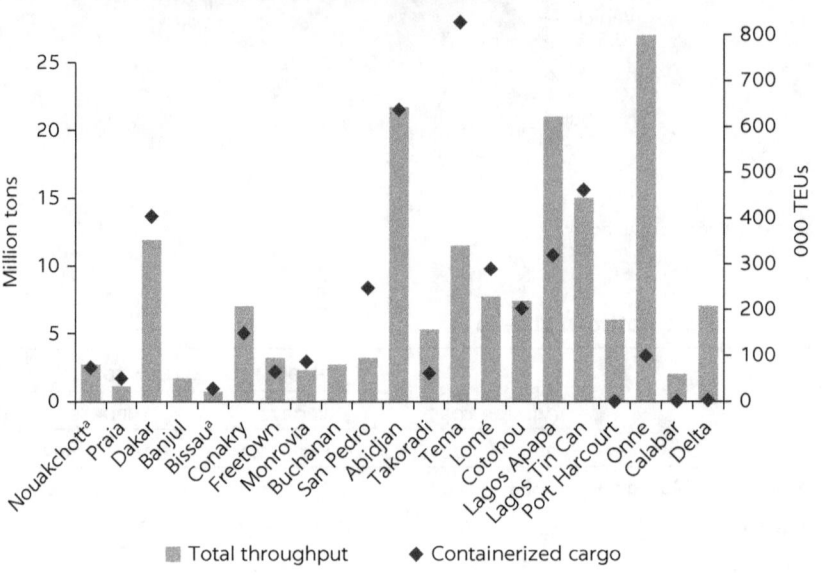

Source: World Bank, 2016b.
Note: TEU = twenty-foot equivalent unit.
a. 2010 data.

landlocked countries such as Mali and Burkina Faso. According to regional standards, Freeport of Monrovia is a small port (figure 3.4).

Freeport of Monrovia is reaching capacity. Although the data may be outdated, they indicate that the average container dwell time is 15 days, and the average duration of vessel stay is minimal (figure 3.5), indicating that port operations are efficient, but that the volume of traffic or vessels may be exceeding available capacity at the port.

Liberia imports a significant amount. Merchandise imports account for approximately 100 percent of GDP, significantly higher than in other sub-Saharan African countries, which normally import 30–50 percent of GDP. As the country's economy recovers from the Ebola crisis, it is likely that Liberia will import more goods and equipment (figure 3.6). Therefore, it is necessary to examine the possibility of expanding the capacity of Freeport of Monrovia or using other ports that are underused.

As the economy picks up and imports increase, it will become more important than ever to keep the port-city interface efficient at Monrovia. As shown above, Liberia exports approximately 6 million tons of goods and imports approximately 2 million tons of goods every year. This generates significant demand for

FIGURE 3.5
Port performance indicators at selected African ports

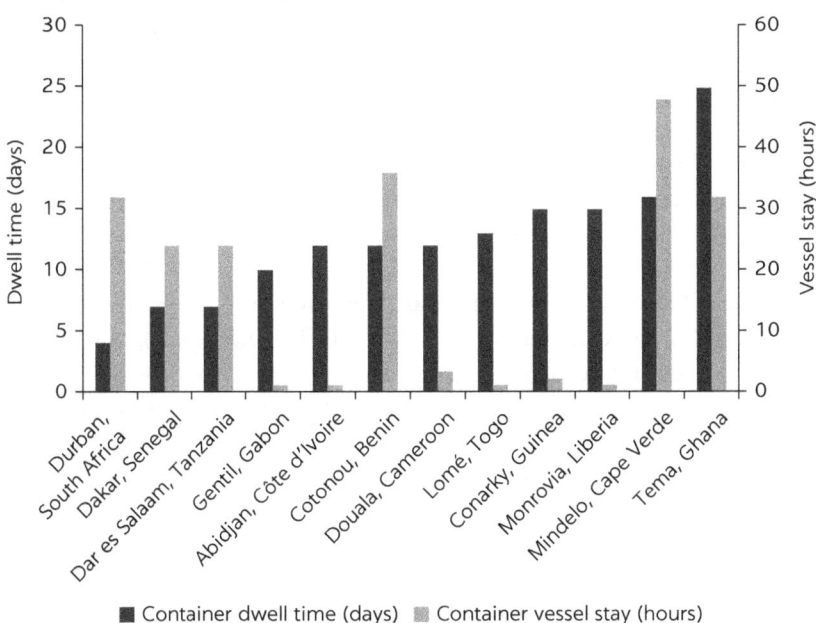

Source: Africa Infrastructure Country Diagnostic database.

FIGURE 3.6
Africa: imports and economic growth

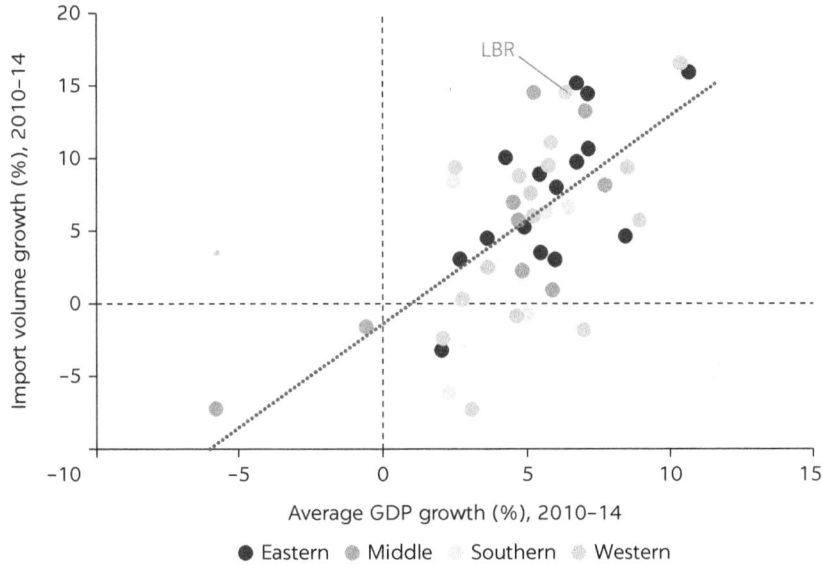

Source: World Bank estimate based on World Development Indicators.

transportation from and to ports. Under the simple assumption that each articulated truck carries 17 tons of goods, some 500 articulate trucks depart from the ports every day. These trucks go to Monrovia and the rest of the country, distributing imported goods and equipment across Liberia.

To examine inland connectivity around and to the ports, transport costs and times are estimated using the same method as above. The assessment here is focused on Freeport of Monrovia because of its operational dominance in the nonmining freight sector. Given the size of the city, and for logistics and consolidation purposes, Freeport of Monrovia is likely to continue to be the primary seaport in Liberia.

Not surprisingly, port accessibility to Freeport of Monrovia is good around Monrovia and along the Monrovia-Ganta corridor, where estimated transport costs are relatively low (less than US$10 per ton) (map 3.7), but beyond the Monrovia-Ganta corridor, transport costs increase substantially because of poor road conditions. From Monrovia, it is estimated that it costs US$14.2 per ton to ship goods to Ganta (more than 250 kilometers away), US$27.3 per ton to Voinjama in Lofa County (more than 400 kilometers away), US$28.8 per ton to Zwedru in Grand Gedeh County (more than 420 kilometers away), and US$48.4 per ton to Pleebo (more than 650 kilometers away).

For obvious reasons, however, there is a possibility that the southeastern regions could take advantage of other seaports, such as Greenville and Harper. Pleebo and Grand Gedeh County are much closer to the Port of Harper. Economies of scale at port operations cannot be underestimated, but inland transport costs could be much lower if ports other than Freeport of Monrovia are used.

Transport costs to the four major ports are estimated in the same way as above (map 3.8). On average, transport costs would decline by US$13 per ton, or

MAP 3.7

Transport costs to Freeport of Monrovia

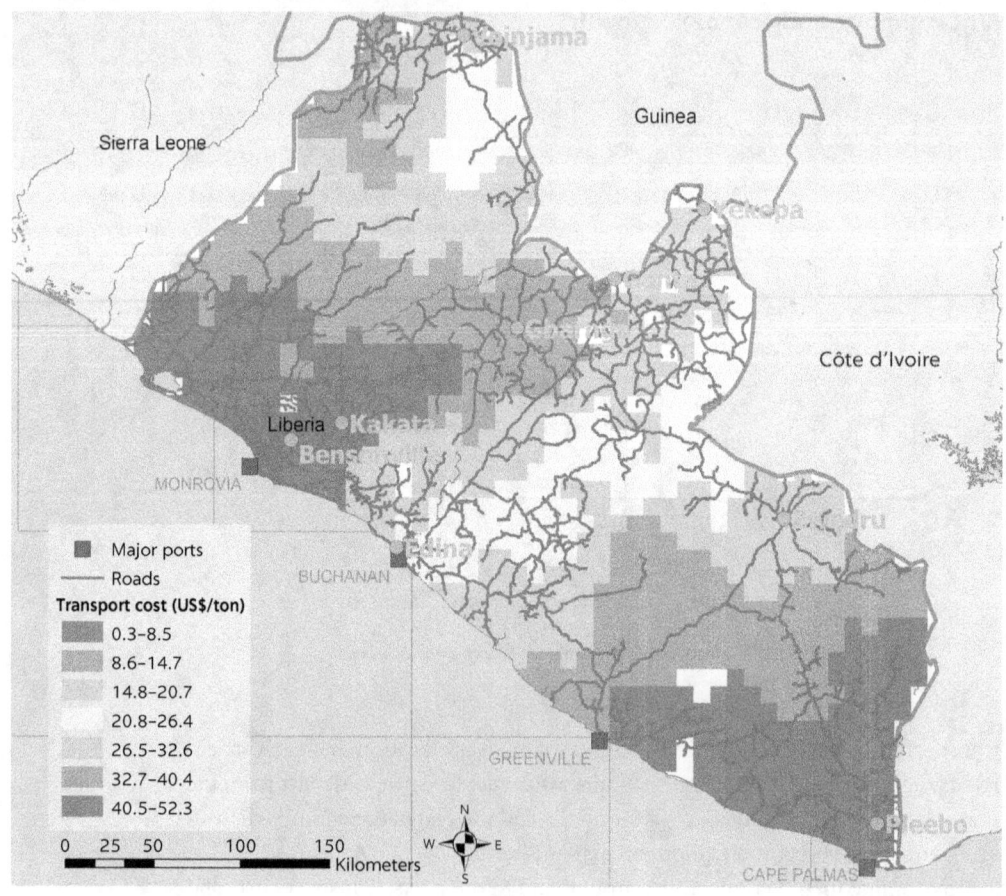

Source: World Bank estimate.

MAP 3.8
Transport costs to four major ports

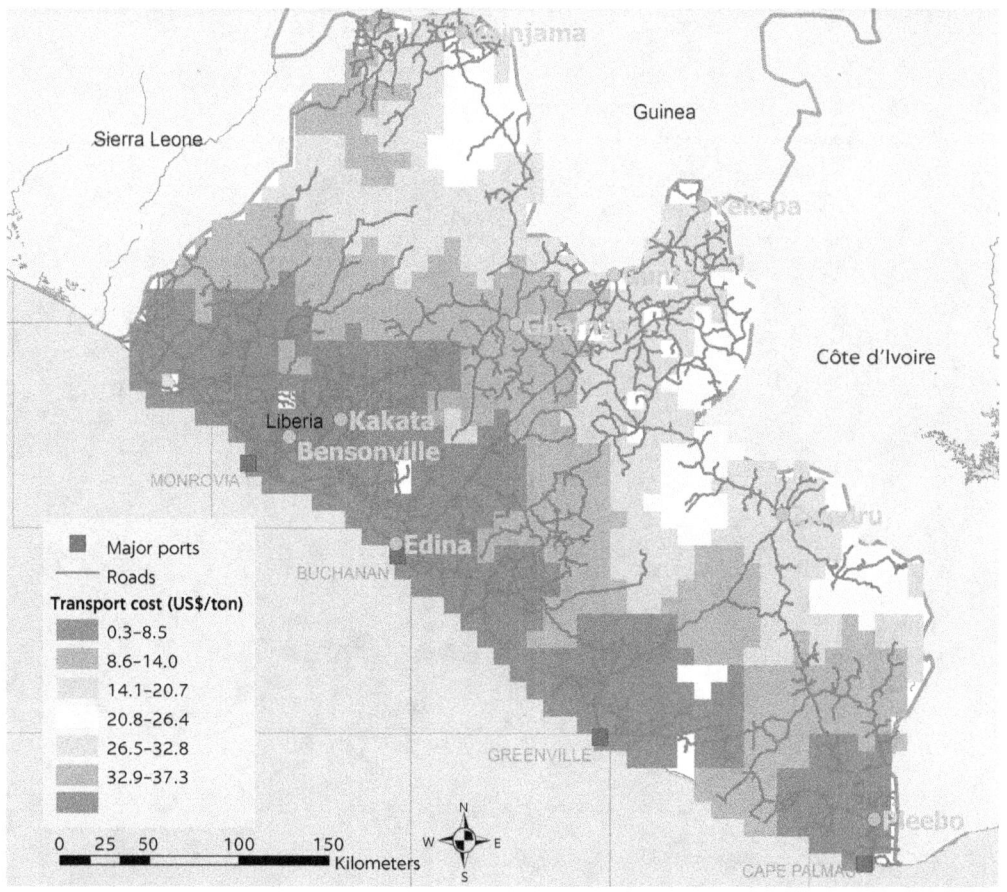

Source: World Bank estimate.

40 percent, mainly in the southeastern regions (map 3.9). This might generate significant economic benefits to the country, as long as individual port operations are financially and economically sustainable. Inland transport connectivity outside of ports, which determines demand for maritime transportation, influences the economic viability of the ports. The areas that Greenville and Harper would service are smaller, primarily because of their poor inland connectivity (map 2.4).

From the end user point of view, Liberians generally have good access to a port. Approximately half the total population lives within 2 hours of Freeport of Monrovia (table 3.5) largely because of the high population concentration in Monrovia. A significant number of people are less than 30 minutes from a port. Two-thirds of the total population lives 4 hours from Freeport of Monrovia. There seem to be significant constraints to connecting people to the port beyond that level. Port access does not decrease proportionally with travel time (figure 3.7). It is estimated that it takes approximately 10 hours to reach the farthest areas from Freeport of Monrovia, such as Pleebo.

A significant number of people could benefit from better access to ports if the other three ports were used more effectively. Purely from a geographic point of view, it is advantageous to think of port access to Harper and Greenville ports from Grand Gedeh, Grand Kru, and Maryland Counties. Ganta and Yekepa could

MAP 3.9
Change in transport costs taking Buchanan, Greenville, and Harper into account

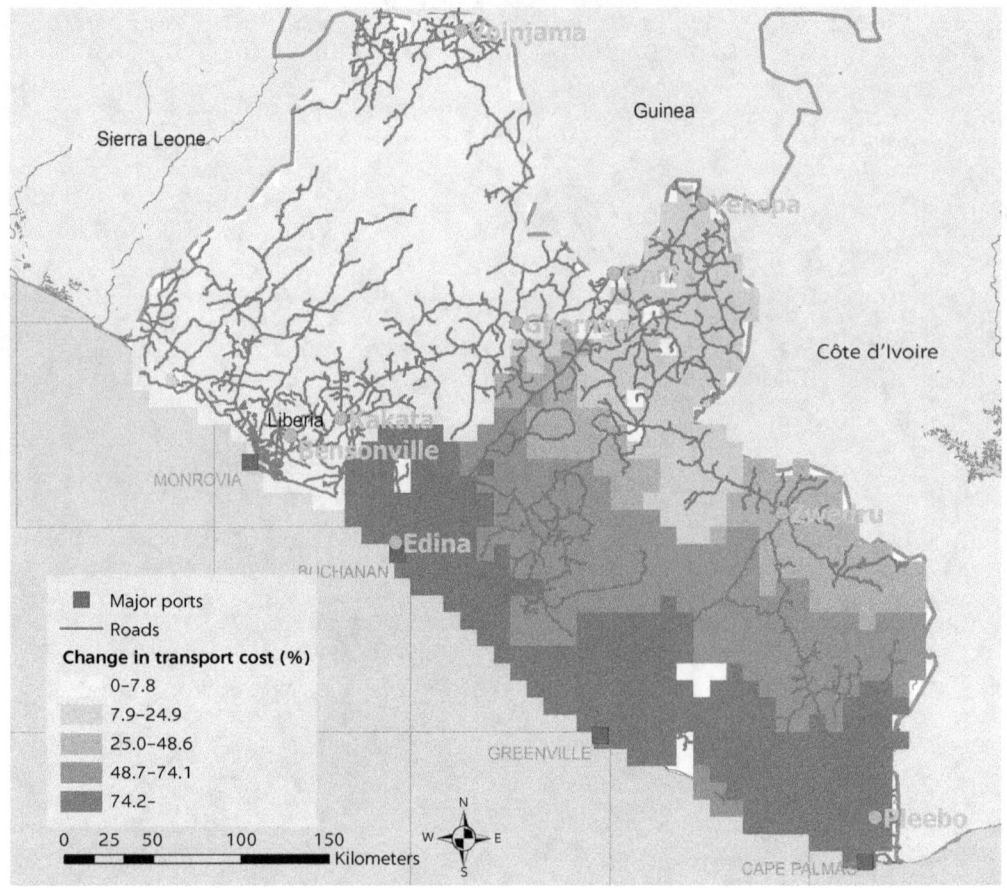

Source: World Bank estimate.

TABLE 3.5 **Population with access to a port**

TRAVEL TIME	TO FREEPORT OF MONROVIA		TO 4 MAJOR PORTS	
	POPULATION (1,000)	% OF TOTAL POPULATION	POPULATION (1,000)	% OF TOTAL POPULATION
Less than 30 minutes	1,369	31.7	1,616	37.4
30 minutes–1 hour	322	7.4	474	11.0
1–2 hours	425	9.8	683	15.8
2–3 hours	366	8.5	518	12.0
3–4 hours	387	9.0	443	10.3
4–5 hours	330	7.6	274	6.3
5–6 hours	297	6.9	114	2.6
6–7 hours	115	2.6	57	1.3
7–8 hours	214	5.0	131	3.0
8–9 hours	107	2.5	10	0.2
9–10 hours	110	2.5	—	—
More than 10 hours	195	4.5	—	—

Source: World Bank estimate.
Note: — denotes that the information is unavailable as of publication date.

FIGURE 3.7
Share of population according to port access

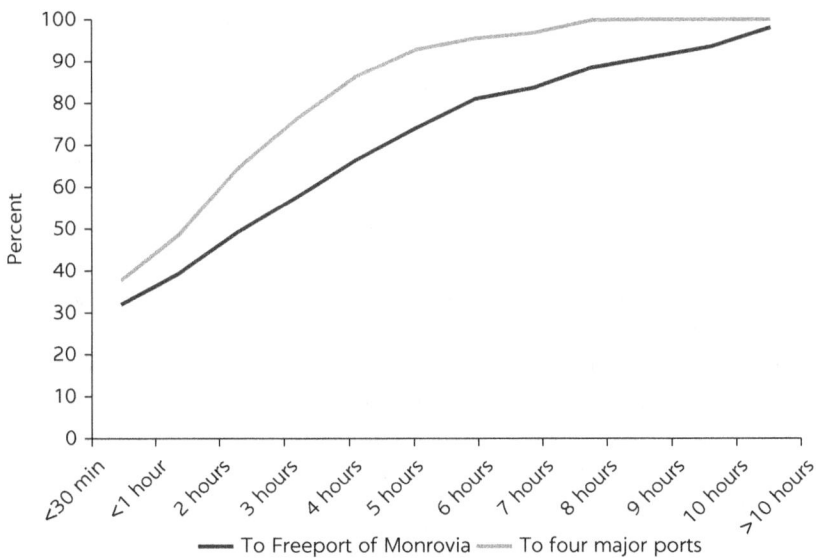

Source: World Bank estimate.

be better connected to the Port of Buchanan, rather than Monrovia, because Buchanan is 30–50 kilometers (approximately 20 percent) closer to them.

If the four ports are taken into account, nearly 90 percent of the total population could have port access at less than 4 hours. Given the limited inland road connectivity, it may make sense to develop other transport modes connecting the seaports, for example, using cabotage arrangements between Monrovia and other seaports. (See more discussion in the following chapter.)

POSSIBLE OPPORTUNITIES TO DEVELOP CABOTAGE

Integrated, intermodal transportation through cabotage is one of the possible solutions worth evaluating given the fact that Liberia's urban population lives in the port cities of Monrovia, Buchanan, Greenville, and Harper and there is limited road transport connectivity in inland areas. Maritime cabotage is generally referred to as movement of goods or passengers between two ports or places within the same state in a country.

There are two main reasons for promoting cabotage over road transport. First, negative externalities of road transport, such as congestion and air pollution, can be reduced if there is a significant modal shift in favor of maritime transport. Second, in many instances, maritime transport offers potentially cheaper freight rates than overland or air shipment. It is often very costly to maintain road assets that can quickly deteriorate when traffic is heavy. Maritime cabotage through international operators can also foster competitiveness in the transport service market, while domestic operators often monopolize road transport.

Unlike other modes of transportation, cabotage can be operationalized by utilizing existing maritime infrastructure or with little augmentation. There may be potential for developing cabotage at a low cost, especially where existing infrastructure is underutilized. From the shippers' point of view, cabotage operations can be easily accommodated. In many countries, a large number of foreign-registered ships call at more than one domestic port. However, they are often prohibited from taking advantage of these journeys to transport domestic cargo between the domestic ports. Therefore, potential cost savings already exist.

Different countries develop cabotage in different ways,[7] but certain policies and administrative interventions are required or of particular use. These include (a) formation of a maritime administration and safety agency, which governs the maritime law for operation and enforcement of cabotage; (b) formulation of a coastal and inland shipping act, which defines the mechanism for applicability of cabotage law; (c) operational waivers for vessels wholly owned or manned or built in the country (in this case, Liberia); and (d) provision of situational variables, such as price incentives that induce switching modes from road to sea, for example, "ecotax" or a rebate on short sea shipping rates. The inclusion of external costs by introducing subsidies may be important to effectively change the financial and social position of short cabotage services (Medda and Trujillo 2010) otherwise road transport will continue to maintain its competitive advantage.

From the infrastructure point of view, the current port capacities in Liberia seem to allow certain developments of cabotage (table 3.6), although detailed engineering feasibility studies need to be undertaken while taking into

TABLE 3.6 **Physical characteristics of major ports in Liberia**

	FREEPORT OF MONROVIA	BUCHANAN	GREENVILLE	HARPER
Quay length	600 m	559 m	400 m	150 m
Land area	18 ha.	—	—	3.73 ha.
Draft	11 m	11.5 m	9.4 m–10 m	5.5 m
Anchorage depth	12.5–13.7 m	14–15.2 m	12.5–13.7 m	9.4–10 m
Cargo pier depth	7.1–9.1 m	9.4–10 m	4.9–6.1 m	11–12.2 m
Oil terminal depth	7.1–9.1 m	9.4–10 m	4.9–6.1 m	n.a.
Dry dock	Small	n.a.	n.a.	n.a.
Harbor size	Small	Very small	Very small	Very small
Railway size	Large	Small	n.a.	n.a.
Harbor type	Coastal Breakwater	Coastal Breakwater	Coastal Natural	Open Roadstead
Maximum vessel size	Over 500 ft in length	Over 500 ft in length	Up to 300 ft in length	n.a.
Ship repair	Limited	Limited	n.a.	n.a.
Annual capacity (1,000 TEU)	75	80	—	41
Pilotage facilities	Yes	Yes	—	—
Tug assist	Yes	Yes	—	—
Lift and crane availability	25–49 ton lifts	0–24 ton lifts	25–49 ton lifts	n.a.
	0–24 ton lifts	Fixed cranes	n.a.	n.a.
	Fixed cranes	Mobile cranes	n.a.	n.a.
	Mobile cranes		n.a.	n.a.

Source: World Bank survey.
Note: — denotes that the information is unavailable as of publication date; n.a. = not applicable.

consideration current levels of service of operational activities, maritime activities demand assessment, port expansion plans, interest of private developers and operators, and investment timeframe for all the ports for planning and implementation of maritime cabotage.

Freeport of Monrovia is protected by two rock breakwaters approximately 2,300 meters and 2,200 meters long, enclosing a basin of 300 hectares of protected waters. The marginal wharf or main pier is 600 meters long and capable of berthing three to four ships, depending on the vessel size. The port also has three finger piers: Liberia Mining Company (LMC), National Iron Ore Company (NIOC), and Bong Mines Company (BMC), which has already been rehabilitated by China-Union Investment. The port handled 386 vessels in 2014.

The Port of Buchanan is 272 kilometers southeast of Monrovia. It is the second-largest port in Liberia. The port's harbor is protected by two breakwaters, 1,890 meters and 590 meters long. Inside the basin, a 225-meter-long iron ore loading quay is located adjacent to the commercial loading quay, providing a water depth of 10.5 meters below chart datum. Adjacent to the loading quay another waiting berth for iron ore carries is available. On the inner side of the secondary breakwater is a commercial quay, 334 meters long with available water depth of 9.5 meters below chart datum. The access channel to the port provides ships a water depth of 11.5 meters below chart datum and a channel width of 210 meters between the breakwaters. In recent times, shipping activities have increased in Buchanan because of increased log export by logging companies and transshipment activities by ArcelorMittal.

The Port of Greenville, which is eight to nine meters below chart datum, is located in Sinoe County in southeastern Liberia about 674 kilometers from Freeport of Monrovia. The Port of Greenville harbor is protected by a 400-meter-long breakwater and on its inner side by two quays. There are two berthing sections: 70 meters and 180 meters, respectively. The Port of Greenville has been a major facility for the export of logs. Several logging agreements are expected to take effect soon, including iron ore and oil palm concessions that will enhance trade and lead to an increase in vessel traffic.

The Port of Harper is located in the southeastern region of Liberia, near the border with Côte d'Ivoire, about 762 km from the Port of Monrovia. The port was constructed on the Rocky Russwurn Island by connecting the island to the mainland by a causeway and by constructing a 150-meter-long breakwater. Berthing facilities are provided by a 100-meter-long reinforced pier with available water depth of 5.5 meters on both sides. Activities at the Port of Harper are centered on the export of logs and sawn timbers from the southeastern hinterland.

From an institutional point of view, various laws need to be formulated to govern cabotage operation through intense discussions with the stakeholders associated with the system. This should be done to introduce clarity and simplify the implementation, operational, enforcement, and monitoring procedures. First, a regulatory authority needs to be established for implementation and enforcement of cabotage administration and safety. This agency will also be responsible for management and operation of the fund to be set up for cabotage operation. Since the movement of passengers and goods shall be limited to domestic connectivity, the framework will require enabling coordination with the National Port Authority, security and immigration services, and custom services in order to empower the cabotage enforcement unit.

Second, a coastal and inland shipping act governing cabotage needs to be prepared. The act will facilitate domestic coastal trade and promote the development of an indigenous network. The provisions shall include restrictions, waivers in order to meet lack of capacity, and enforcement amongst others. The act will be governed by a legislative framework to restrict access or reserve maritime trade to indigenous capacities within the geographical space of the country.

In addition, restrictions and waivers may need to be established and enforced. This is a policy decision of how the cabotage market is intended to be developed. While it can allow any foreign or domestic vessel to engage in cabotage operations, it is a possibility that vessels other than those wholly owned and manned by a citizen of the country in question and built and registered in the country of operation, are restricted from the domestic coastal carriage or cargo and passengers within the coastal territorial, inland waters, island or any point within the waters of the Liberian Economic Zone. Customs and border protection and other enforcement agencies need to collaborate with each other to enforce the preferences.

The authority should be given powers under the act to grant waivers to foreign vessels to participate in cabotage trade when it is satisfied that local operators lack the capacity to carry the volume of business associated with the cabotage. A waiver request would include the purpose for which the waiver is sought, port(s) involved, and estimated period of time for which the waiver is sought.

Thus, vessel registration is key for implementation of cabotage. Global experiences with vessel registration and cabotage are cited in box 3.1 below. The Liberian Registry is open to any ship owner in the world and accepts any type of vessel so long as it meets the registry's standards. The pre-registration formalities are user-friendly and designed to meet international standards in relation to safety and documentation, and to protect the interests of ship owners registering their vessels in Liberia.

Safety is another important regulation for developing cabotage. Liberia is a signatory to all the major safety, security, and environmental protection conventions and treaties. As an active and involved member of the International Maritime Organization (IMO), Liberia has set the standard with regard to IMO participation and early ratification of the major safety and environmental protection treaties. The Maritime Safety Department under Liberian Registry (LISCR) is responsible for:

Verification of the security plan implementation
Verification of the safety management system implementation
Evaluating vessel compliance through inspections and audits, and by reviewing reports
Developing and ensuring minimum safe manning requirements
Oversight of the Liberian Nautical Inspectors and International Safety Management (ISM) and International Ship and Port Facility Security (ISPS) Code Auditors
Responding to requests concerning the ISM code
Managing appeals concerning port state detentions or other control actions
Issuance of manning dispensations
Management of the duty officer program.

Fiscal regimes can be used to support cabotage operations. In the European Union, for example, the fiscal regime applicable to a ship engaged in international maritime cabotage in the EEA is set by the state in which the ship is registered. The principal fiscal elements provided include: corporate tax relief of various forms (but increasingly in the form of a low-rate tonnage tax) and a

> **BOX 3.1**
>
> ## Global Experiences with Vessel Registration and Cabotage
>
> The European Union has been able to apply access to national cabotage to all member states as a minimum requirement in the European Economic Area (EEA). In practice, seven European states—Belgium, Denmark, Iceland, Ireland, the Netherlands, Norway, and the United Kingdom—have chosen not to place any restrictions on foreign flag access. Of these seven countries, four (Belgium, Iceland, Ireland, and the Netherlands) have very low levels of both cargo and passenger cabotage activity. While Denmark's cabotage trade is somewhat more significant, it has been contracting in size. Only the United Kingdom and Norway have significant cabotage tonnage, both in terms of cargo and passengers.
>
> Of the states that have restrictions on foreign vessels, these constraints take a variety of forms. In Finland, foreign vessels are generally prohibited from entering domestic coastal trades, except under a permit issued when no suitable Finnish flag vessel is available. France and Germany also prohibit the use of foreign flag vessels except under a waiver system. These waivers may be granted if no EEA vessels are available or where they are available under "very unfavorable" conditions. Waivers can also be granted on the basis of reciprocity, for example, to Greece.
>
> Italy and Portugal restrict cabotage to EEA flag shipping and lay down "host state" rules for EEA ships' crews in the applicable trades. The Ministry of Transport Navigation may grant waivers on a case-by-case basis.
>
> There are certain cases where crew nationality is required. Most EEA states require that the ship's master be of the nationality of that ship's ownership state, whereas others extend the requirement to certain other officers. For example, France, Italy, Portugal, and Spain require the first officer to be a national as well. In certain instances, but not in all circumstances, there is a waiver system. For example, there is no flexibility in this requirement for the ship's master in Sweden or Greece, whereas in the United Kingdom the master of certain vessels that are designated "strategic ship types" must be a British national or a citizen of a Commonwealth, EEA or NATO member state.
>
> However, with regard to crewing, the normal requirement for first registers is for the crew to be citizens of EEA member states. However, certain states (e.g., Denmark) authorize engagement of third-country nationals in their first register so long as they are engaged under terms equivalent to seafarers of that state. Certain states that also have second registers may authorize nationals to be engaged under local wage conditions (e.g., Denmark).

significant degree of tax relief for crews on income and social security benefits. However, it is important to keep administrative procedures to the minimum. Many administrative and inspection requirements relating to maritime cabotage are due to the fact that the authorities make no distinction between domestic movement of cargo and international trade. Checks by the agencies responsible for safety and immigration, the agricultural service, and the police, among others, should be more flexible in the case of cabotage and possibly also in the case of trade with countries that form part of the same economic bloc.

ACCESS TO SOCIAL FACILITIES

Reliable transport infrastructure is essential to ensure connectivity to social facilities such as health care centers and schools. Given the recent Ebola crisis, this is of particular importance in Liberia. To assess accessibility to health care facilities, georeferences of health care facilities were recorded along with the road inventory survey.

Six hundred and eighteen health care facilities were mapped: 34 hospitals, 56 health centers, and 528 health clinics (table 3.7). Health facilities are located all over the country, including in remote areas. Hospitals and health centers are typically located in county capitals. Health clinics exist in most districts (map 3.10).

Many people seem to have access to basic health services at least at the clinic level, but access to a higher level of services is limited. In Liberia, people have at least one health facility within 20 kilometers of their home. Using the global population distribution data, WorldPop, it is estimated that approximately 90 percent of the total population has access to a health facility within 10 kilometers (table 3.8). Approximately 40 percent have access within 2 kilometers (figure 3.8).

Access to the higher level of health services provided at hospitals and health centers is more limited; only 15 percent of the total population lives within 2 kilometers of a hospital. Approximately 40 percent of the total population does not have any hospital within 20 kilometers of their home. Availability of doctors and medical supplies and access to higher levels of health services are a challenge in rural Liberia.

Different types of transport connectivity may be needed to ensure access to health facilities. Two strategies are examined to identify critical road links. First, the country's health supply depends heavily on foreign aid, so to provide adequate health care services, it is important to connect major health facilities (hospital or health center) to Monrovia, from where all medical equipment and supplies are distributed. To this end, approximately 2,674 kilometers of roads are identified as important supply routes (map 3.11). Most of them are primary roads, including the Monrovia-Ganta and Harper-Voinjama corridors.

TABLE 3.7 **Number of health facilities mapped**

COUNTY	CLINIC	HEALTH CENTER	HOSPITAL
Bomi	23	1	1
Bong	40	—	2
Gbarpolu	15	—	1
Grand Bassa	30	3	3
Grand Cape Mount	29	3	1
Grand Gedeh	17	3	1
Grand Kru	11	4	1
Lofa	48	4	4
Margibi	23	8	2
Maryland	22	3	1
Montserrado	149	18	11
Nimba	55	6	4
River Gee	17	3	—
Rivercess	16	—	1
Sinoe	33	—	1
Total	528	56	34

Source: World Bank survey.
Note: — denotes that the information is unavailable as of publication date.

MAP 3.10
Location of health facilities

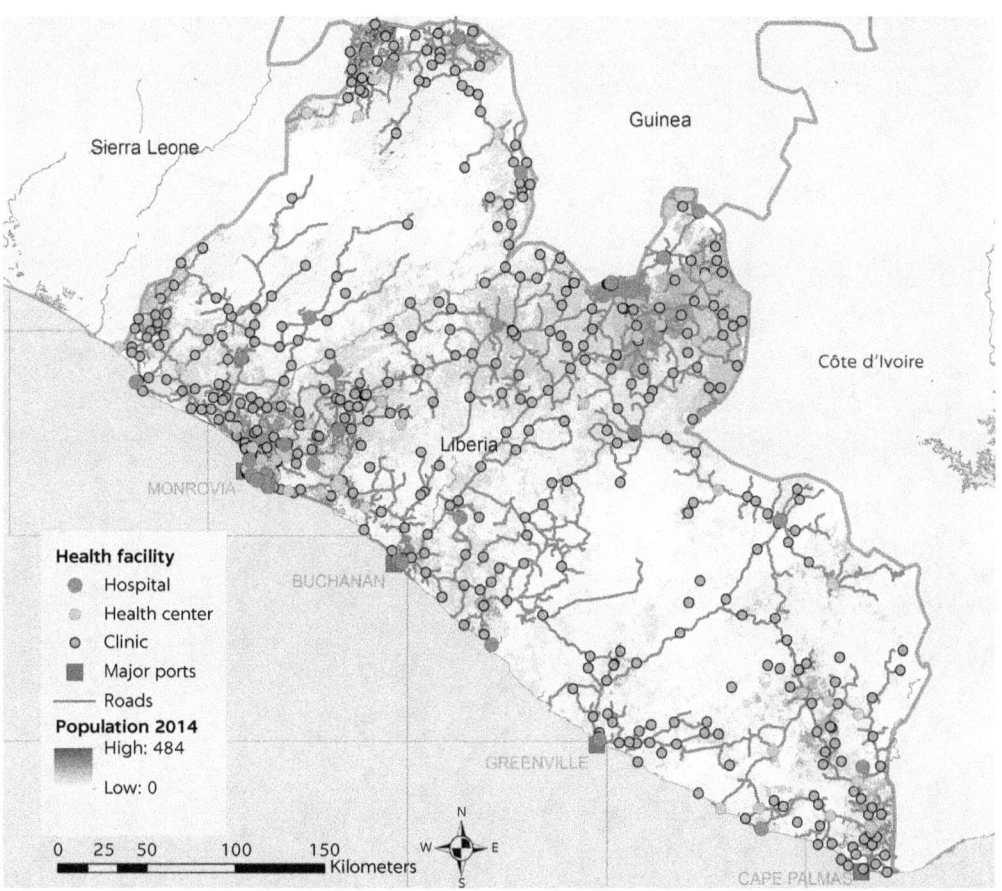

Source: World Bank survey.

TABLE 3.8 **Population with health care access**
Millions

DISTANCE (KM)	HOSPITAL	HOSPITAL OR HEALTH CENTER	HOSPITAL OR HEALTH CENTER OR CLINIC
2	0.68	1.24	1.86
5	1.33	1.80	2.86
10	1.90	2.40	3.91
20	2.57	3.34	4.33

Source: World Bank estimate.

This confirms the importance of improving and maintaining the primary road network.

To ensure this level of connectivity, some 1,100 kilometers of roads still need to be improved. Of these priority routes, approximately 600 kilometers (20 percent) are in excellent or good condition (table 3.9); 1,160 kilometers are in poor or very poor condition and need to be rehabilitated.

Due to these poor roads, only 30 of 89 major facilities are considered to be well connected to Monrovia (map 3.12). This is assessed based on the proportion of roads in excellent, good, or fair condition along each route to Monrovia. As an example, the threshold is set at 80 percent: a facility is considered to be connected if more than 80 percent of roads that are used to go to that facility are

FIGURE 3.8
Share of population with health care access

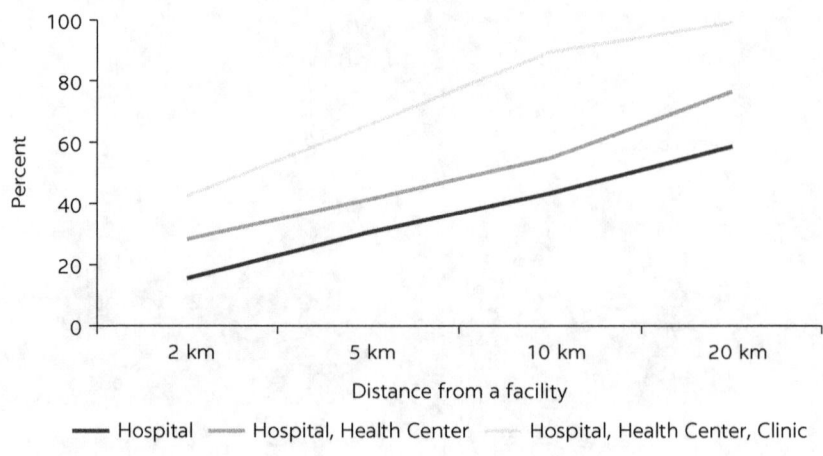

Source: World Bank estimate.

MAP 3.11
Key routes from Monrovia to hospitals

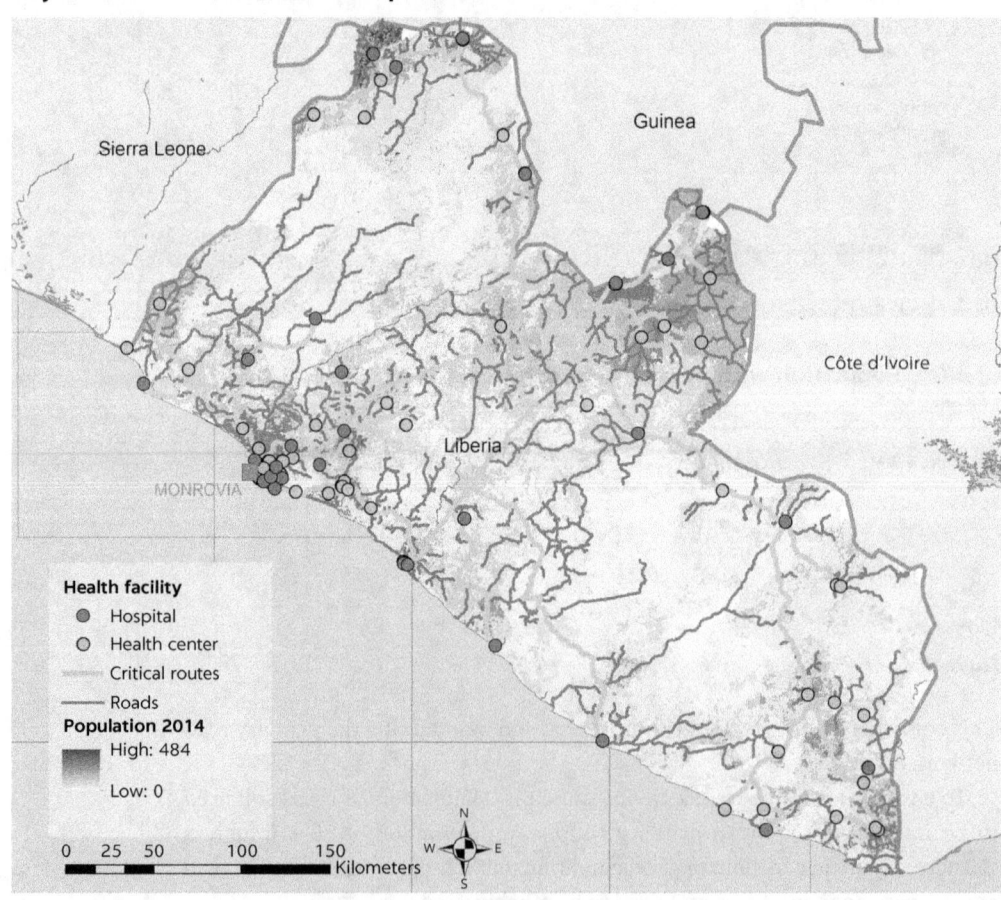

Source: World Bank estimate.

TABLE 3.9 **Priority roads identified for health service accessibility**

TARGET CONNECTIVITY	LENGTH (KM)	OF WHICH:				
		EXCELLENT	GOOD	FAIR	POOR	VERY POOR
From Monrovia to hospitals and health centers	2,766	432	176	1,000	981	178
District capitals to hospitals and health centers	2,808	273	111	1,110	1,028	286

Source: World Bank estimates.
Note: Sums may not add up perfectly due to rounding.

MAP 3.12
Health facility connectivity to Monrovia

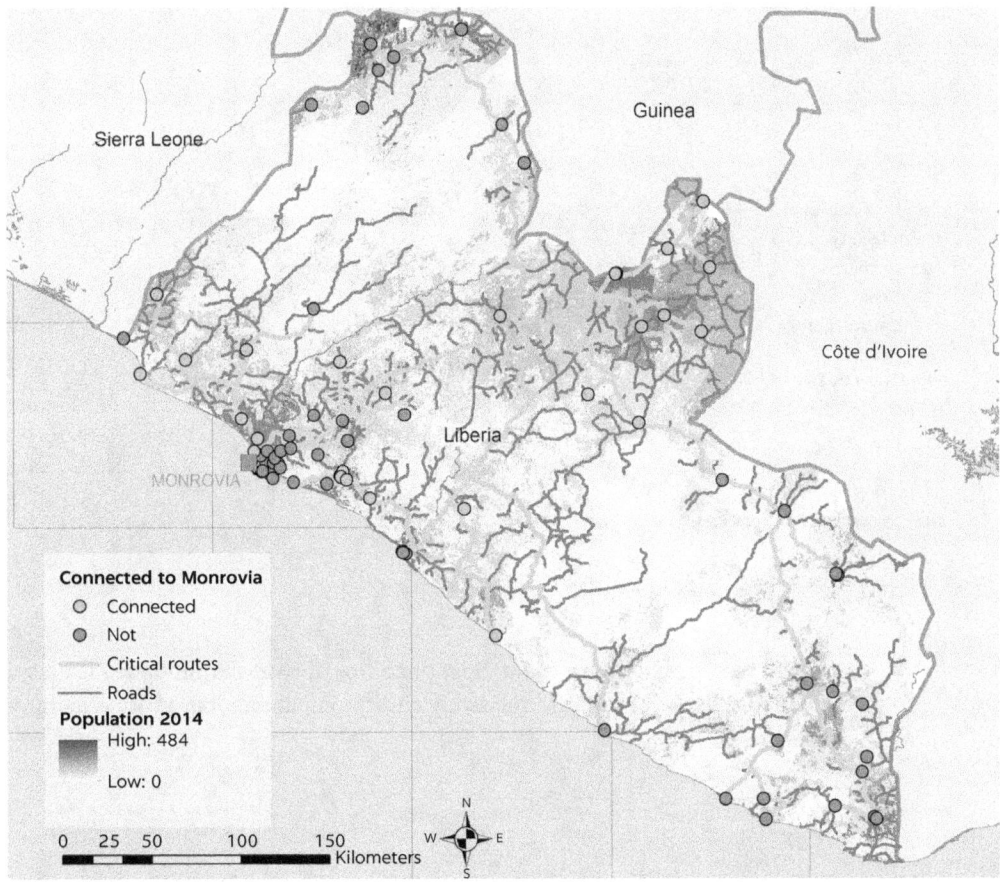

Source: World Bank estimates.

in good condition. There are many unconnected facilities around Monrovia that are close to the city but cannot be accessed with good roads, reflecting the poor condition of secondary and feeder roads around Monrovia. Many hospitals in Lofa County and the southeastern regions are also unconnected because of poor inland road connectivity from the north to the south, as discussed above.

Second, from the point of view of more local access, another priority may be to connect communities (represented by district capitals) to major health facilities. To this end, approximately 2,800 kilometers of roads are identified as a priority (map 3.13). This is even more challenging than the first scenario because most of these roads are unpaved feeder roads and nearly half of them are in poor or very poor condition (table 3.6). Significant resources will be

MAP 3.13
Key routes from districts to hospitals

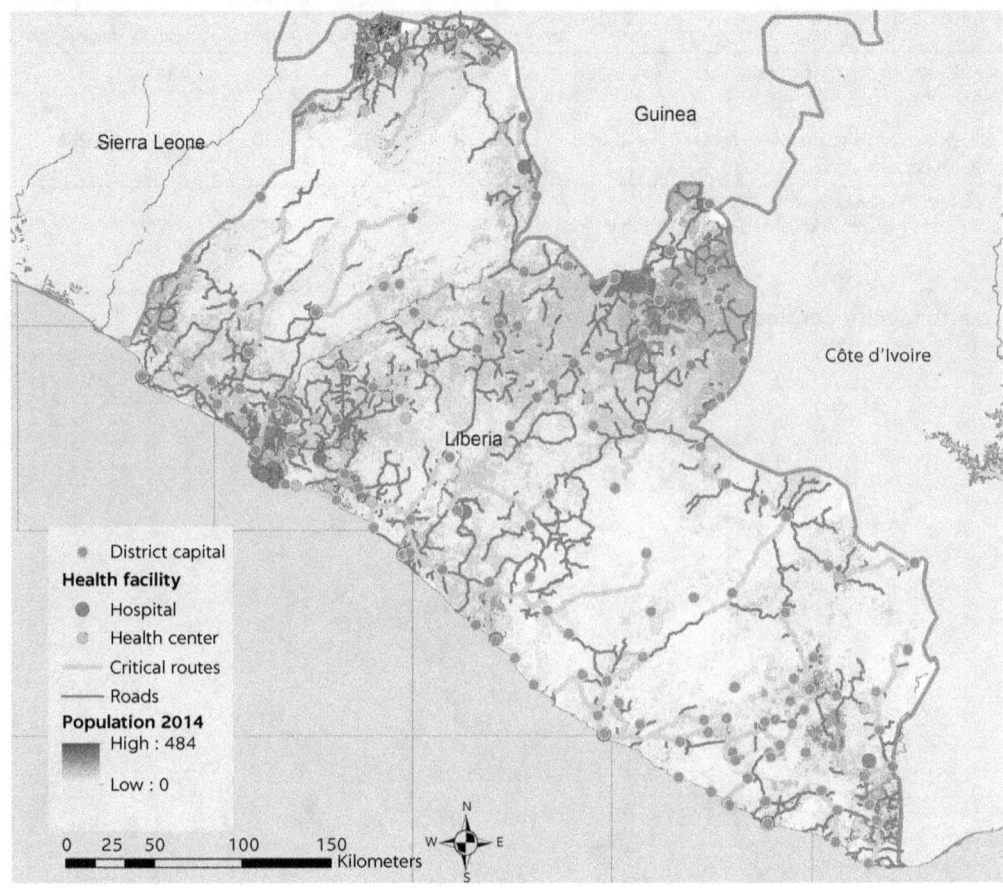

Source: World Bank estimate.

required to rehabilitate them. Sustainability of road maintenance is also a challenge. Gravel roads are relatively cheap to maintain, but routine maintenance is critical.

NOTES

1. These were supported by two World Bank-financed projects: Liberia Road Asset Management Project and Liberia Urban and Rural Infrastructure Rehabilitation Project.
2. Absolute poverty is defined as a situation where individuals cannot meet their food and non-food minimum needs. The benchmark for those needs is established through an overall or absolute poverty line and is defined as the line below which individuals cannot meet their food and non-food minimum needs.
3. See more detailed discussion in LISGIS 2017.
4. According to the Public Expenditure Review conducted in 2013, approximately 70 percent of government capital expenditures are dedicated to roads and bridges. Based on the International Monetary Fund's projection, capital spending would amount to US$230 million in 2017. Liberia's GDP is approximately US$2 billion.
5. Unit costs are assumed to be US$1 million for paved roads and US$75,000 for unpaved roads.
6. The literature also uses negative exponential weights. See, for instance, Elbadawi, Mengistae, and Zeufack 2006; Lall and Mengistae 2005.
7. See appendix A for some detailed discussion in two countries: Brazil and Nigeria.

REFERENCES

Elbadawi, Ibrahim, Taye Mengistae, and Albert Zeufack. 2006. "Market Access, Supplier Access, and Africa's Manufactured Exports: An Analysis of the Role of Geography and Institutions." World Bank Policy Research Working Paper 3942, World Bank, Washington, DC.

Holl, Adelheid. 2004. "Manufacturing Location and Impacts of Road Transport Infrastructure: Empirical Evidence from Spain." *Regional Science and Urban Economics* 34 (3): 341–63.

Lall, Somik V. and Taye Mengistae. 2005. "The Impact of Business Environment and Economic Geography on Plant-Level Productivity: An Analysis of Indian Industry." World Bank Policy Research Working Paper 3664, World Bank, Washington, DC.

Limão, Nuno, and Anthony Venables. 2001. "Infrastructure, Geographical Disadvantage, Transport Costs, and Trade." *The World Bank Economic Review* 15 (3): 451–79.

LISGIS. 2017. Liberia Institute of Statistics & Geo-Information Services. Household Income and Expenditure Survey 2016 Statistical Abstract.

Medda, Francesca, and Lourdes Trujillo. 2010. Short-sea shipping: an analysis of its determinants. Maritime Policy & Management, Vol. 37(2), pp 285–303.

Procher, Vivien. 2011. "Agglomeration Effects and the Location of FDI: Evidence from French First-Time Movers." *Annals of Regional Science*, Vol. 46: 295–312.

Roberts, Peter, K. C. Shyam, and Cordula Rastogi. 2006. "Rural Access Index: A Key Development Indicator." *Transport Papers* TP-10. The World Bank Group, Washington, DC.

UNCTAD (United Nations Conference on Trade and Development). 2015. *Review of Maritime Transport 2015*. New York: UNCTAD.

Wilmsmeier, Gordon, Jan Hoffmann, and Ricardo J. Sanchez. 2006. "The Impact of Port Characteristics on International Maritime Transport Costs." *Research in Transportation Economics: Port Economics* 16: 117–40.

World Bank. 2016a. *Measuring Rural Access: Using New Technologies*. Washington, DC: World Bank.

———. 2016b. *Making the Most of Ports in West Africa*. Washington, DC: World Bank.

4 Broader Transport Connectivity

INTERMODAL CONNECTIVITY

As discussed, one of the clear challenges in Liberia is limited road transport connectivity in inland areas, especially between the north and south. Inland road transport costs are high—for instance, approximately US$50 per ton from Freeport of Monrovia to Pleebo or Harper (map 3.7). It might be possible to overcome this by developing other transport modes and enhancing intermodal connectivity. Current economic activity and freight traffic, except for mineral exports, are highly concentrated in Monrovia. Other ports may be able to contribute to efficient movement of goods and people by being connected differently.

Cabotage

Integrated intermodal transportation through cabotage could be one solution. Sixty percent of Liberia's urban population lives in the port cities of Monrovia, Buchanan, Greenville, and Harper. Significant economic benefits could be achieved by more efficiently connecting the four cities. Maritime transport costs are generally lower than road and rail transport costs. Maritime transport costs can be 60 percent lower than rail and 80 percent lower than truck transportation costs (TRB 2002). In the case of Liberia, the cost differential may be even greater because the north can be connected to the south more directly using cabotage, and the condition of the roads is poor.

Cabotage has the potential to dramatically reduce transport costs between Monrovia and the other major coastal cities. Maritime transport costs are assumed to be one-third the average road cost, which is US$0.029 per ton-km.[1] Transport costs from Monrovia to Buchanan, Greenville, and Harper could be reduced by some 80 percent (table 4.1 and map 4.1), and the transport distance would be up to 200 kilometers less.

Economic benefits could be significant in inland areas of the southeastern counties. Transport costs could be reduced by 10–30 percent over large areas (map 4.2). For instance, cabotage between Monrovia and Harper would reduce shipping costs to Zwedru, the capital of Grand Gedeh County.

TABLE 4.1 **Transport costs to Monrovia with cabotage**

DESTINATION	TRANSPORT COST ($/TON)		CHANGE (%)
	ROAD ONLY	WITH CABOTAGE	
Buchanan	24.7	3.4	−86.4
Zowieta	14.2	14.2	−0.1
Ganta	14.2	14.2	−0.1
Yekepa	19.6	19.6	−0.1
Greenville	39.9	7.7	−80.8
Zwedru	28.8	24.2	−15.8
Harper	50.2	12.2	−75.7

Source: World Bank estimate.

MAP 4.1
Transport costs to Monrovia with cabotage

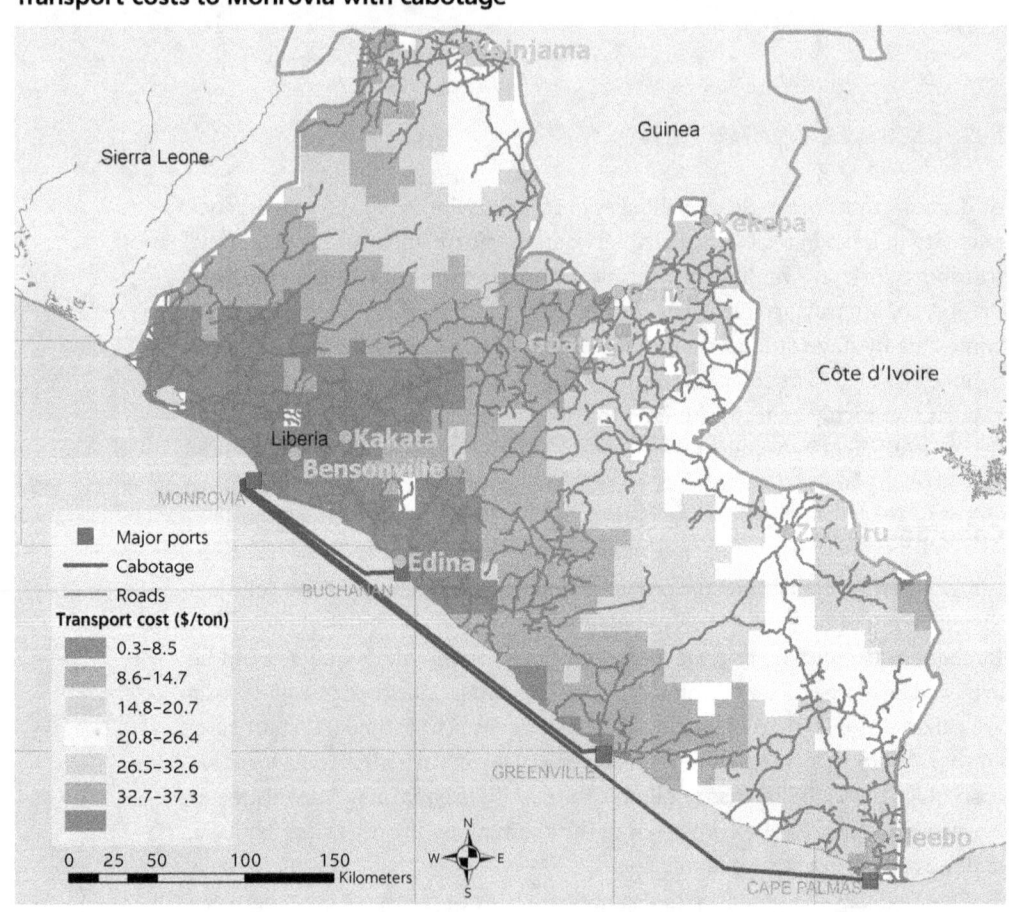

Source: World Bank estimate.

Transport costs to inland areas in Bong and Nimba would not change much because the Monrovia-Ganta corridor has been rehabilitated and is already in good condition. No additional costs that might be incurred at the ports are assumed in this assessment. Efficient and seamless intermodal connectivity is assumed.

MAP 4.2
Reduction in transport costs with cabotage

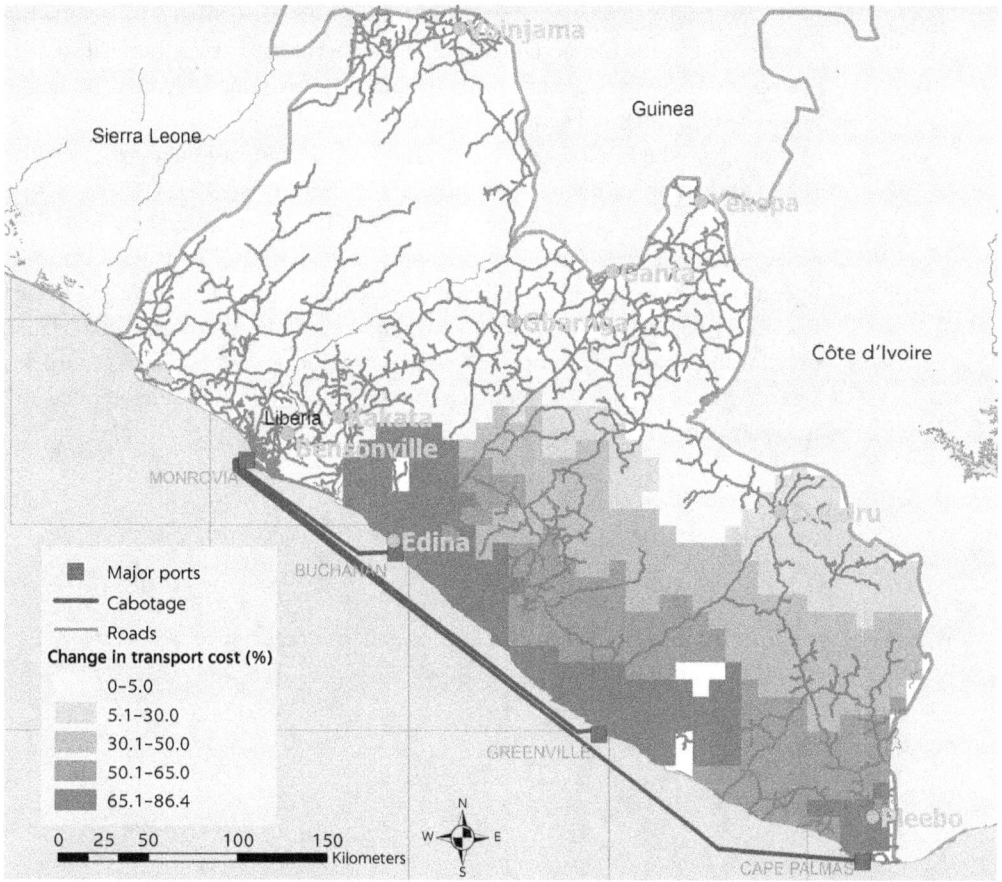

Source: World Bank estimate.

Railroads

Railroads are another important asset. There are three rail lines in Liberia: the Liberian-American-Swedish Mining Company (Lamco) line, Mano River Railway, and Bong Mine Railway. The Lamco rail line, currently operated by ArcelorMittal, extends approximately 270 kilometers from Buchanan to Yekepa, near the border with Guinea. It is operated by a mining company and used exclusively for its mining exports. Operating speed is approximately 60 kilometers per hour. Mano River Railway, which connects the western mining areas in Bomi and Grand Cape Mount Counties to Monrovia, is not operational. Bong Mine Railway is a short connection, 76 kilometers, from Bong Mines to Monrovia. It is operated by China-Union Investment and used exclusively for its iron ore exports. Operating speed is 45 kilometers per hour and no explicit freight charge is set.

From a transport connectivity point of view, the rail lines could be used to ship other goods to inland areas at lower costs. Rail transport generally has an advantage for long-haul shipment. The combination of cabotage and railway could be used to reduce transport costs from Monrovia to inland areas in Grand

Bassa, Nimba, and Grand Gedeh Counties, such as Zwedru, the capital of Grand Gedeh County.

To examine this possibility, transport costs were recalculated to include the Lamco rail line. It was assumed that rail transport costs are two-thirds of average road costs (US$0.057 per ton-km). Four stations are assumed between Buchanan and Yekepa: Botpta, Zowieta, Ganta, and Sanniquellie.

Not surprisingly, using the Lamco rail line to connect inland areas around Ganta to the Port of Buchanan would be beneficial (map 4.3). Transport costs could be reduced by 20–30 percent. The Port of Buchanan would have to be fully operational not only for mining exports, but also other export and import operations. The expected beneficiary areas would be limited to Bong and Nimba Counties (map 4.4) because economic benefits from rail transport materialize only for long-haul shipments, and alternative port access by road (Monrovia-Ganta corridor) is efficient enough; the corridor has just been rehabilitated and is largely in good condition.

MAP 4.3

Transport costs to four major ports with the Lamco rail line taken into account

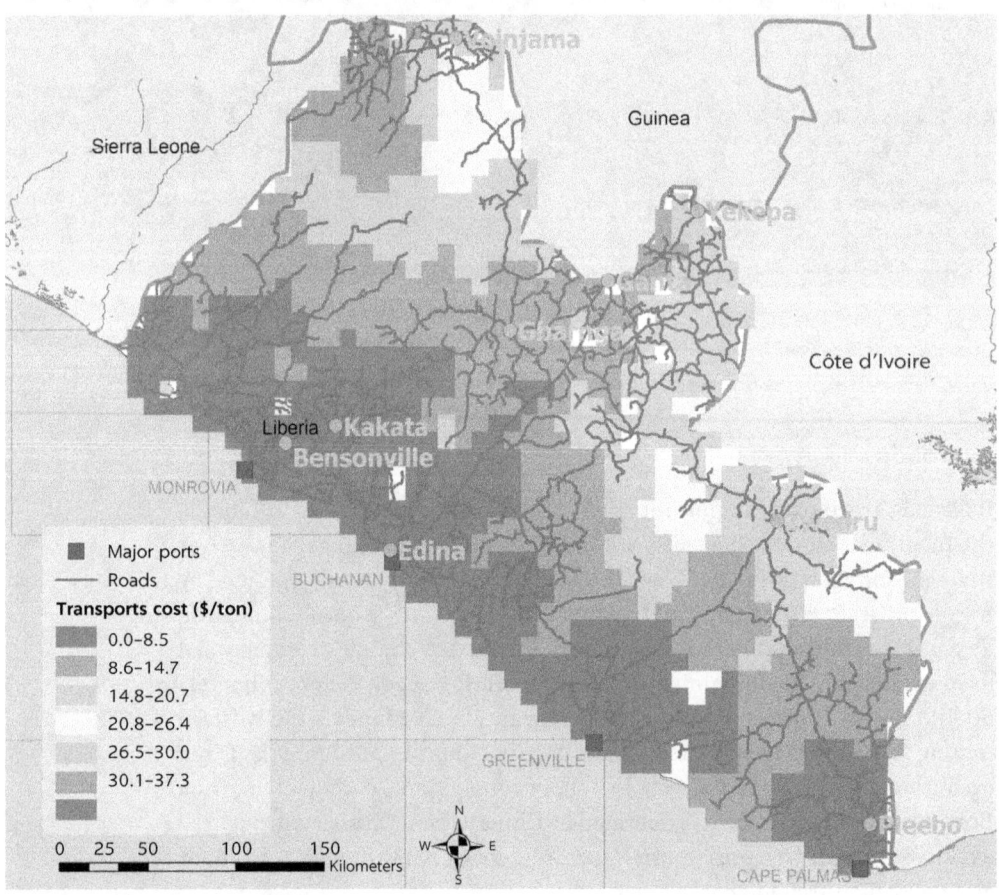

Source: World Bank estimate.

MAP 4.4
Reduction in transport costs with Lamco rail line taken into account

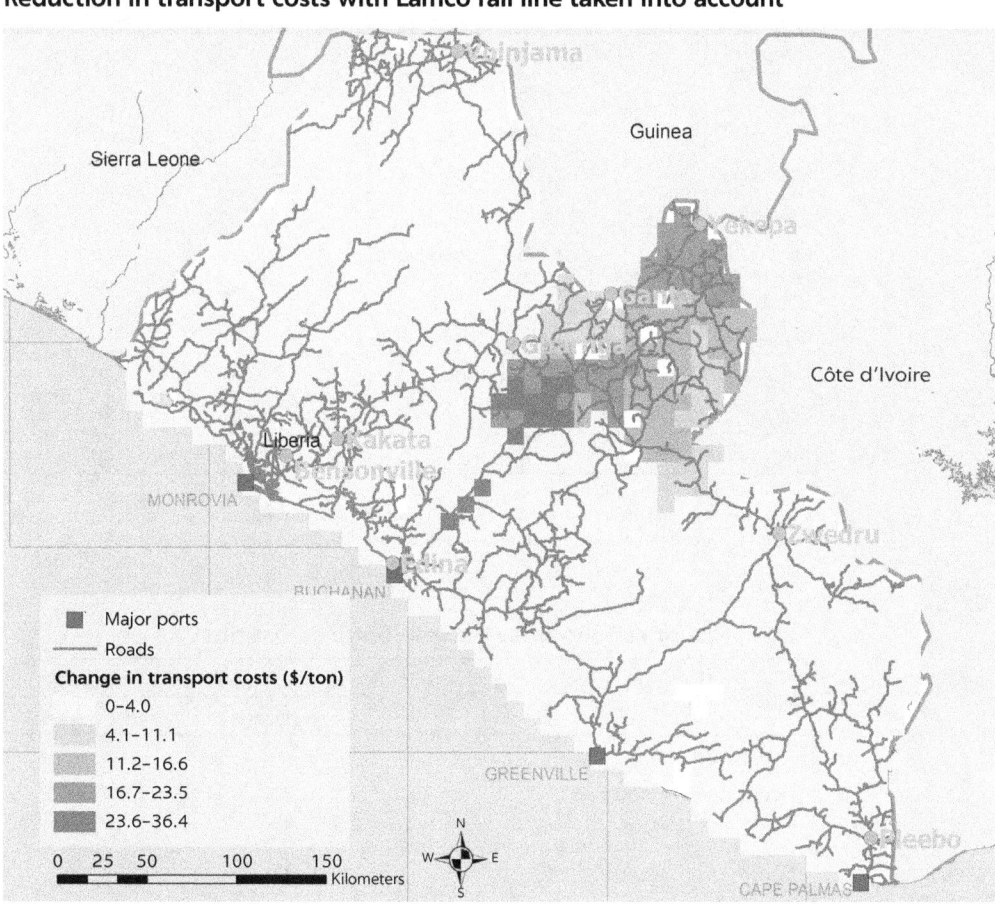

Source: World Bank estimate.

REGIONAL CONNECTIVITY

In general, regional trade and integration is an important development goal to stimulate economic growth. The Trans-West African Coastal Highway, which passes through several West African countries, including Liberia, from Dakar to Lagos, was developed to enhance regional trade and integration in West Africa.

Liberia does not have much regional trade through inland borders. The vast majority of the country's trade takes place at the seaports. According to customs revenue data, Liberia's trade with neighboring countries is a small part of its total trade. Approximately 70 percent of customs revenue is collected at Freeport of Monrovia, followed by Buchanan, which handles iron ore exports (table 4.2). Trade through border crossings with Sierra Leone, Guinea, and Côte d'Ivoire accounts for less than 1 percent of the total and includes agricultural commodities, fish, general consumer goods, and vehicles (table 4.3).

From the regional connectivity point of view, the north-central region around Ganta has potential. Regional accessibility is defined in a similar way to the Market Access Index (MAI), with the populations of

TABLE 4.2 **Customs revenue according to customs office, 2014/15**

CUSTOMS OFFICE	PARTNER COUNTRY	US$ MILLION	SHARE (%)
Freeport	Global	124.30	70.4
Buchanan	Global	3.05	1.7
Ganta	Guinea	0.47	0.3
Greenville	Global	0.42	0.2
Bo Waterside	Sierra Leone	0.33	0.2
Harper	Global, Côte d'Ivoire	0.23	0.1
Yealla	Guinea	0.19	0.1
Loguatuo	Côte d'Ivoire	0.16	0.1
Toe Town	Côte d'Ivoire	0.10	0.1
Other[a]	—	47.2	26.8
Total	—	176.48	100.0

Source: Liberia Revenue Authority.
Note: — denotes that the information is unavailable as of publication date.
a. Including Liberia Petroleum Refining Company and small facilities such as parcel post.

TABLE 4.3 **Major commodities trade at border crossings**

BORDER POINT	AVERAGE MONTHLY VOLUME (TONS)	
	TO LIBERIA	FROM LIBERIA
Ganta (to Guinea)	—	—
Agricultural commodities	12.5	3.5
Cars	15.0	—
Construction material	4.0	—
Rubber	7.5	—
Pig feed	—	5.0
Clothes	—	2.0
Slippers	—	2.5
Other	1.5	4.0
Bo Waterside (to Sierra Leone)	—	—
Fish	1.5	—
Plastic material	—	1.5
Other	4.0	3.5

Source: World Bank consultant survey.
Note: — denotes that the information is unavailable as of publication date.

neighboring countries used as proxies for the potential market. Bong and Nimba Counties are relatively well connected to neighboring countries, especially Guinea and Côte d'Ivoire (map 4.5). Connectivity to Sierra Leone is low.

The rail connectivity to Buchanan is examined to explore regional integration benefits in the inland areas, such as Bong and Nimba Counties. These counties could benefit from improved multimodal connectivity to the Port of Buchanan

MAP 4.5
Regional access index

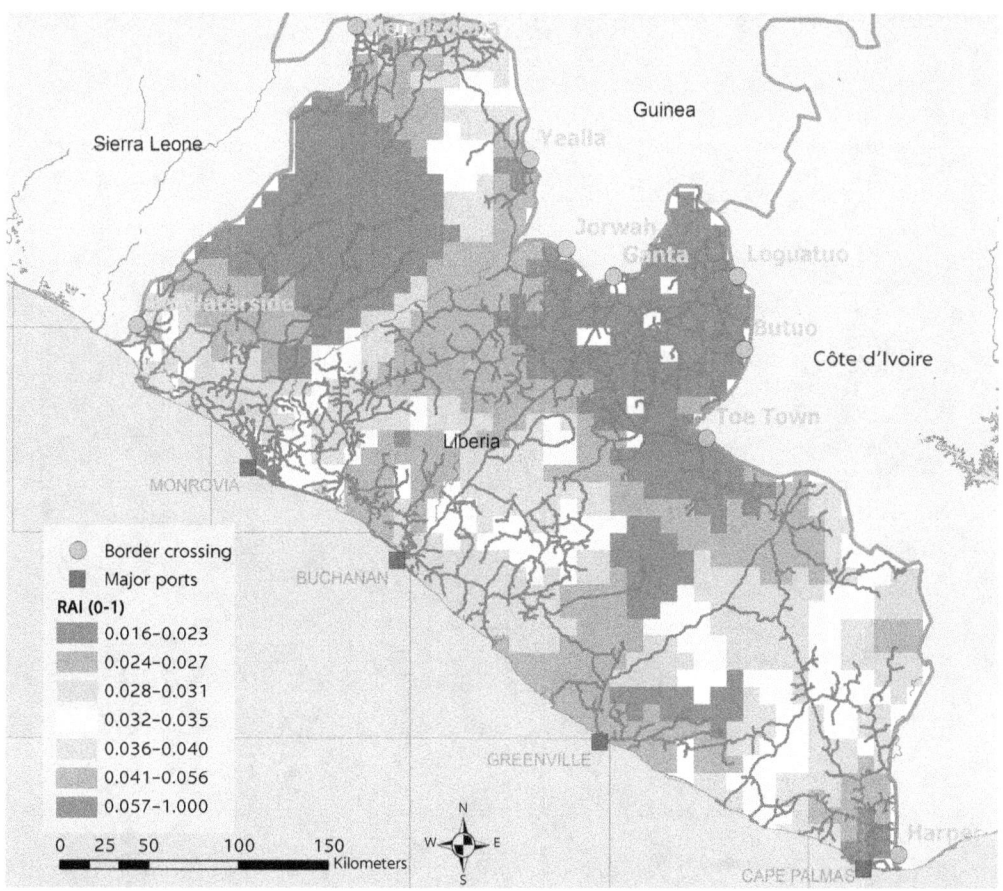

Source: World Bank estimate.

by the Lamco rail line. This could be a useful foundation for supporting trade in the region.

An obvious challenge is that these potential areas are far from Monrovia, but there is significant market potential, with approximately 800,000 people in Bong and Nimba Counties. Agricultural production is significant and there are local businesses in the area. (See the following chapter.) Regional growth could materialize if regional connectivity were increased. Two main corridors are important in this regard: Monrovia-Ganta and Harper-Voinjama (near Mendikorma). Map 4.6 shows key corridors that connect Monrovia to border crossings. These are the best regional corridors, minimizing transport costs given current road conditions.

MAP 4.6
Important roads for regional connectivity

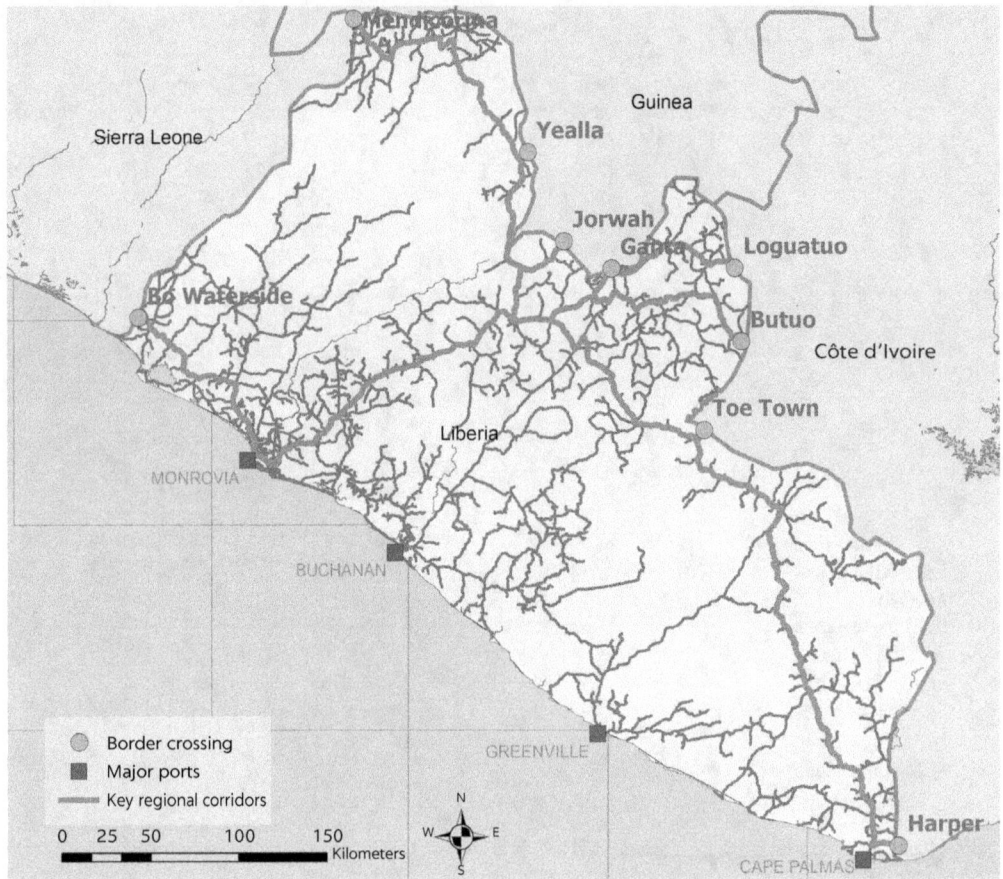

Source: World Bank estimate.

NOTE

1. Road user costs in Liberia are estimated to vary from approximately US$0.05 to US$0.15 per ton-km, depending on road condition, with an average of US$0.086 per ton-km.

REFERENCE

TRB (Transportation Research Board). 2002. "Comparison of Inland Waterways and Surface Freight Modes." TR NEWS 221, TRB. www.trb.org.

5 Potential Economic and Social Benefits from Improved Connectivity

AGRICULTURAL PRODUCTION

Agriculture is an important economic sector in Liberia. Approximately half of the population engages in agricultural production,[1] and approximately US$350 million in crops is produced annually.[2] Cassava, sugarcane, and rice are major crops in Liberia (figure 5.1). Agricultural production is concentrated around Monrovia and Bong County (map 5.1). Grand Bassa and Nimba Counties are also productive. There is another cluster of crop production areas around Harper in the south where food crops such as rice and bananas are produced.

As indicated above, Liberia's agricultural productivity is low. Among others, transport connectivity is an important constraint for farmers. There is significant correlation, although not necessarily causality, between crop production and market accessibility. The correlation coefficient associated with transport costs to a large city is estimated at −0.31 (figure 5.2). When the size of the population is taken into account, the correlation is higher (0.56 in absolute terms) (figure 5.3). This can be interpreted to mean that in order to stimulate agricultural production, access to a market with purchasing capacity, not just a city, is important. In the case of Liberia, the most important market is Monrovia.

Rural accessibility is also necessary for farmers to bring their produce to market. Not surprisingly, there is a high correlation (0.53) between agricultural production value and rural accessibility at the county level (figure 5.4). The greater rural accessibility, the more crop production there is (also see map 3.1). Thus, markets and rural access are essential.

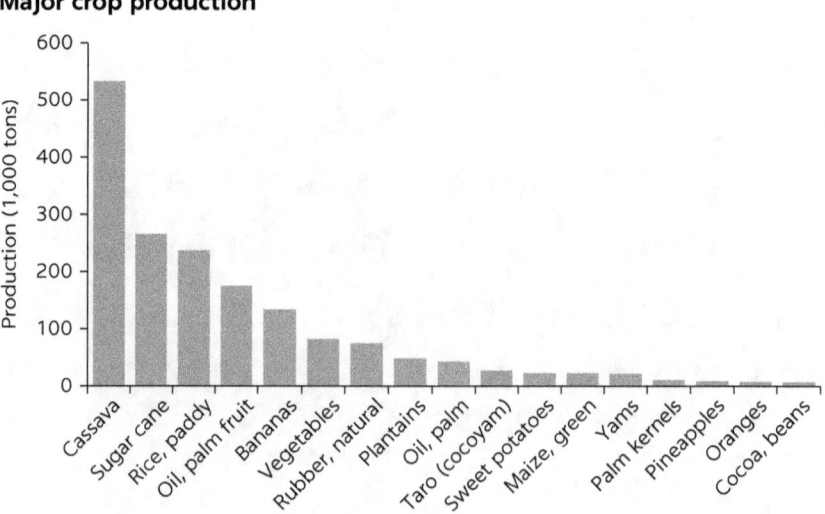

FIGURE 5.1
Major crop production

Source: Food and Agriculture Organization Corporate Statistical Database.

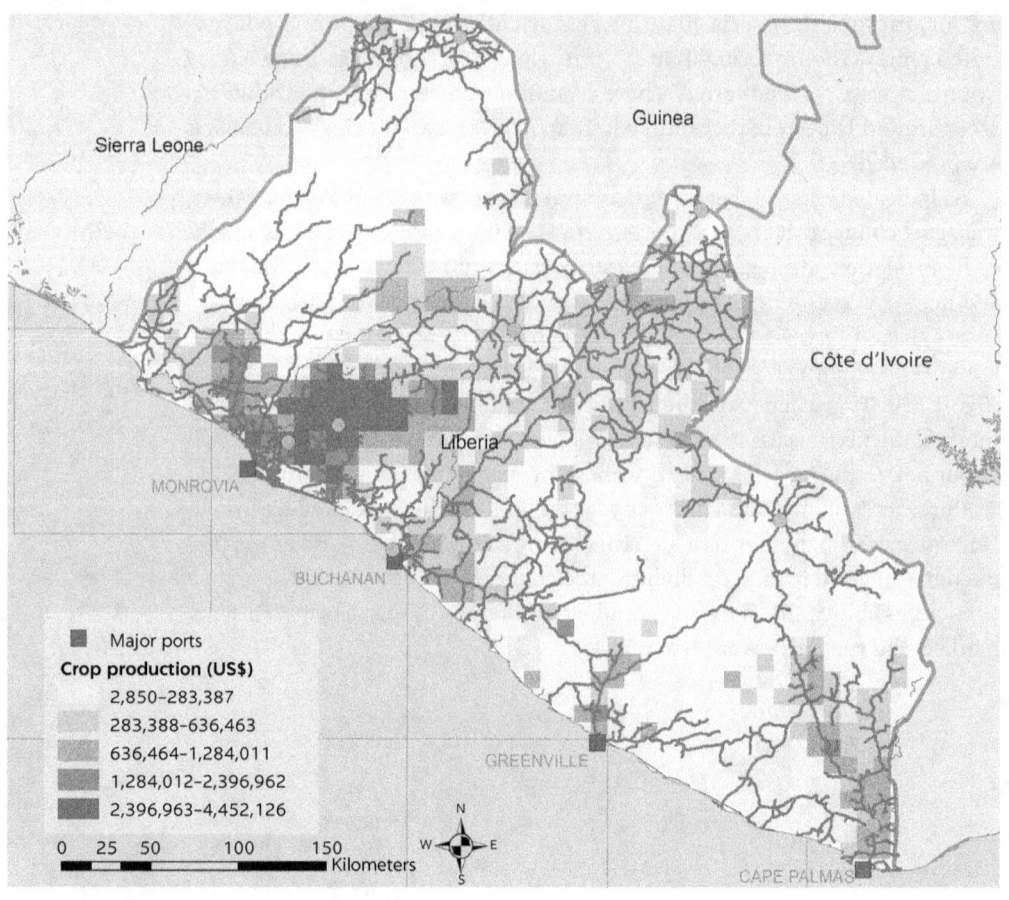

MAP 5.1
Current agricultural production areas

Source: International Food Policy Research Institute spatial production allocation model.

FIGURE 5.2
Transport costs to market and crop production value

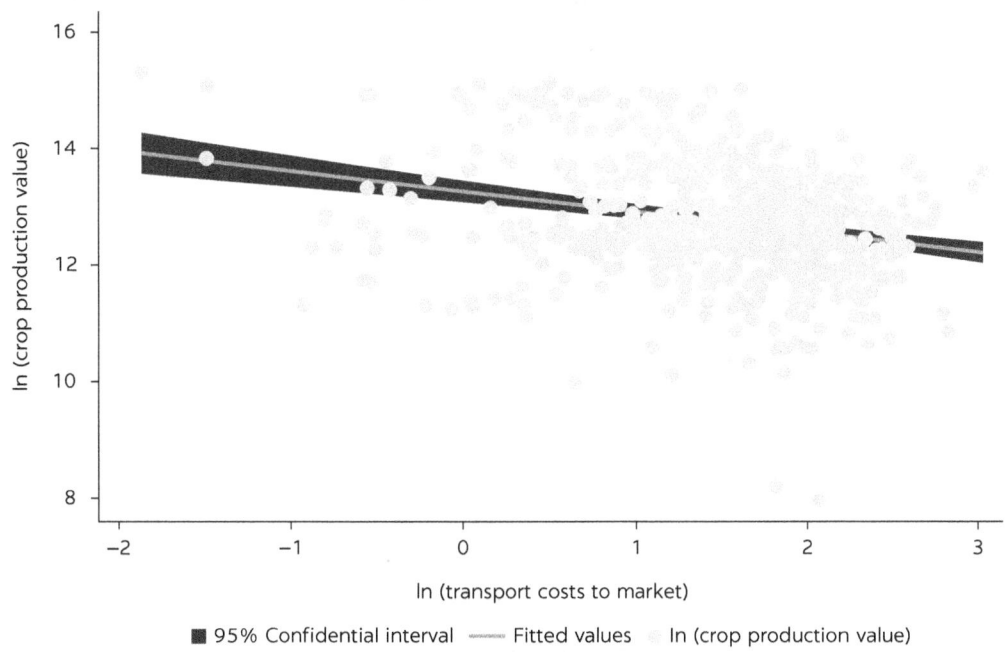

Source: International Food Policy Research Institute spatial production allocation model; World Bank estimate.

FIGURE 5.3
Market access index and crop production value

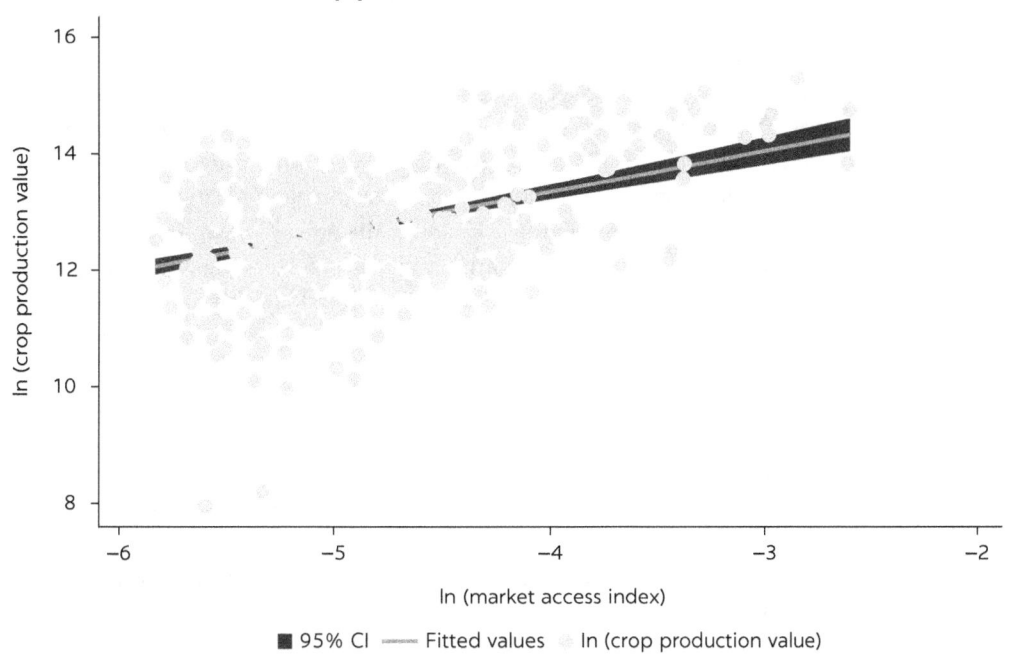

Source: International Food Policy Research Institute spatial production allocation model; World Bank estimate.

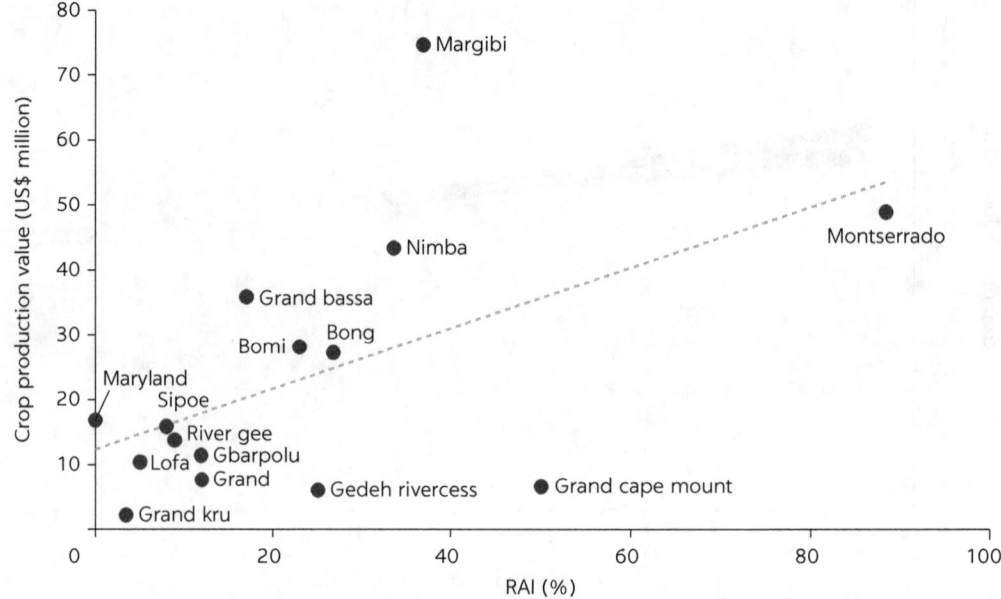

FIGURE 5.4
Correlation between rural access index and crop production

Source: International Food Policy Research Institute spatial production allocation model; World Bank estimate.
Note: RAI = Rural access index.

FISHERIES

Fisheries are another important and perhaps untapped potential sector in Liberia. The country has a 570-kilometer-long coastline. According to the fishery registry database managed by the Bureau of National Fisheries, approximately 9,000 crews, including approximately 3,000 foreign fishermen, engage in fishing activities in the country. Approximately 3,300 canoes are officially registered and operate at more than 100 landing sites, landing some 7,000 tons of fish annually (figure 5.5). According to the Food and Agriculture Organization Global Fishery Production Statistics, the estimated production volume of Liberia is far lower than that of neighboring countries. Liberia and its neighboring countries are fish importers (figure 5.6). Some fish are imported at the border point of Bo Waterside from Sierra Leone (see table 4.3). Therefore, the regional fish market has potential for Liberia if the fishery industry can be boosted.

Since fish are perishable, good rural connectivity from landing sites to markets is essential. In Liberia, there are more than 90 landing sites (which can be clustered into 55 landing areas for analytical purposes), and approximately 1,280 kilometers of roads have been identified as important routes to connect landing sites to markets (with more than 15,000 population) (map 5.2). Most are rural roads along the coastline and are not part of the primary network.

Rehabilitation and maintenance of these roads is likely to be cost effective. Of 1,280 kilometers, approximately 1,000 kilometers are in fair, poor, or very

FIGURE 5.5
Fishery production, 2014

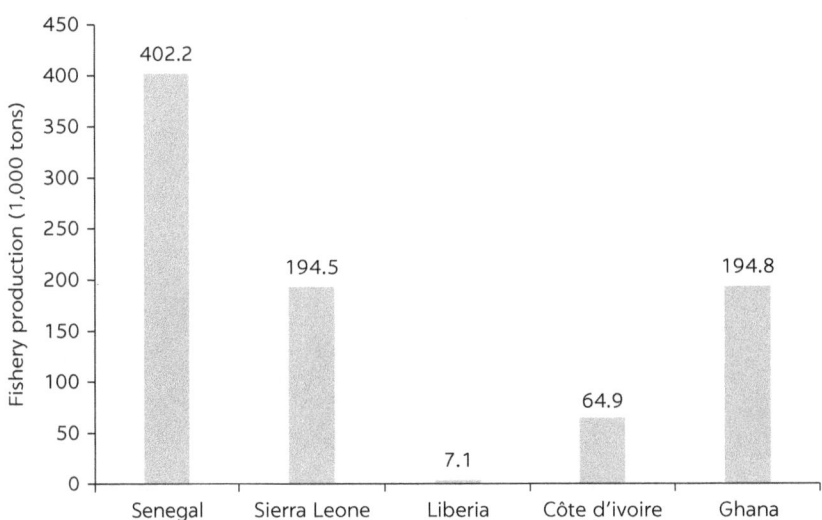

Source: Food and Agriculture Organization Fisheries and Aquaculture Department.

FIGURE 5.6
Fishery trade volume, 2013

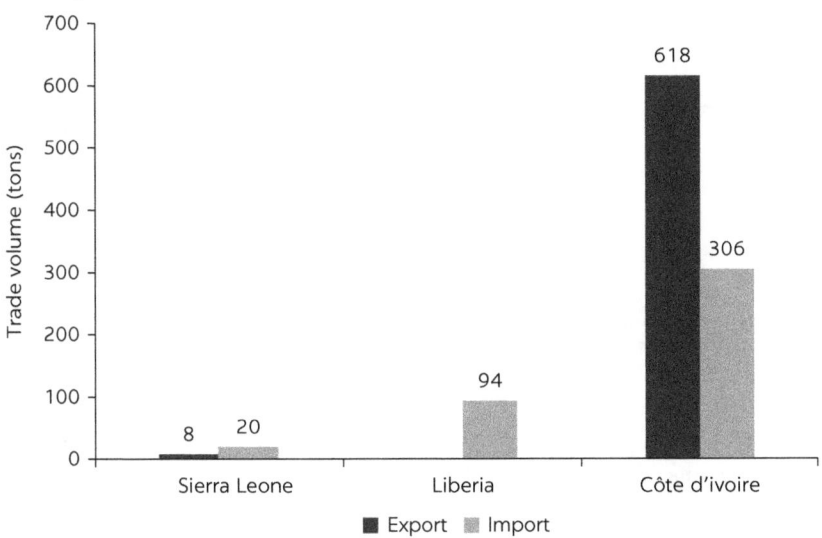

Source: Food and Agriculture Organization Fisheries and Aquaculture Department.

poor condition and need to be improved and maintained (table 5.1). Although further assessment is needed for detailed specifications, these roads are likely to need to meet only the low level of standards, and, therefore, required works will be relatively inexpensive. Yet, a significant number of people could benefit if these feeder roads were improved. It is estimated that approximately 794,000 people live within 5 kilometers of a landing site. Approximately 1.1 million

MAP 5.2
Landing sites and key routes to markets

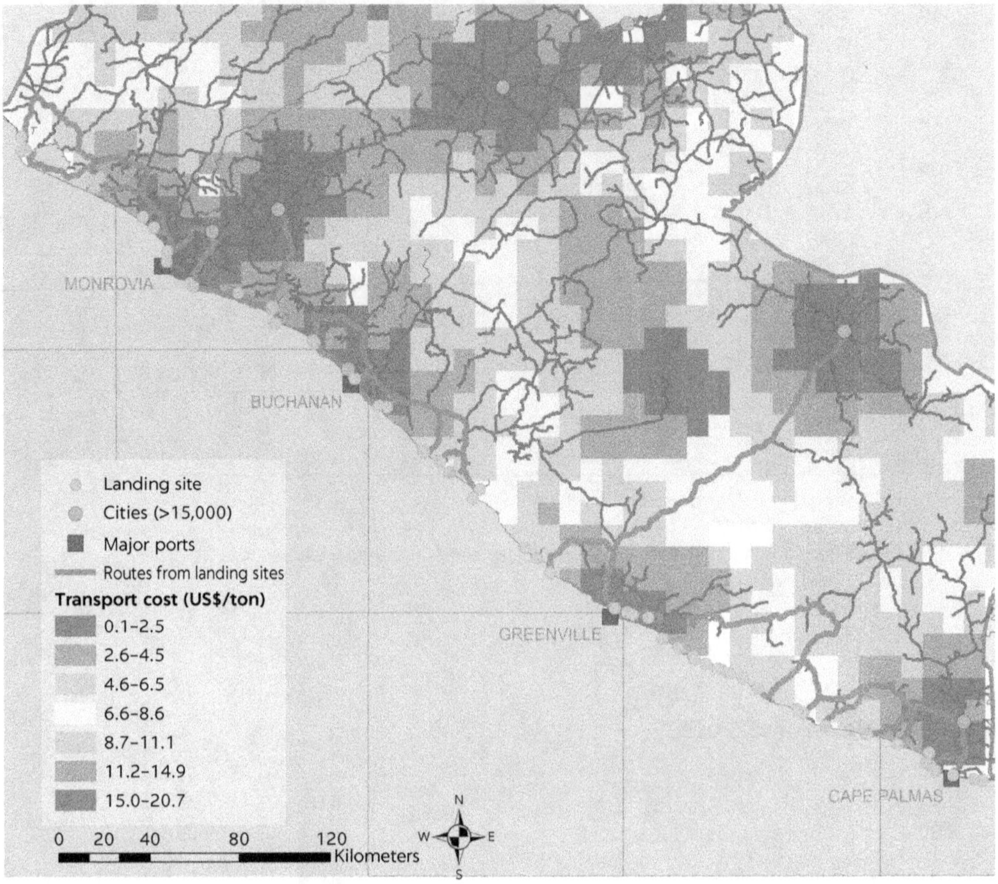

Source: World Bank estimate.

TABLE 5.1 **Condition of key routes from landing sites to markets**

	TOTAL	EXCELLENT	GOOD	FAIR	POOR	VERY POOR
Length (km)	1,284	192	71	454	484	83
Share (%)	100.0	14.9	5.5	35.4	37.7	6.5

Source: World Bank based on data provided by the government of Liberia.

people who live along these key routes are also expected to benefit from improved connectivity. These investments are economically viable.

The statistical relationship between connectivity and fishery outcome is also supportive; it is likely that better transport connectivity would contribute to more efficient distribution of fish and, therefore, encourage more fishery activities. The number of people involved in fisheries is highly correlated with transport costs to a market. Again, the relationship is not necessarily causal, but more people work in the fishery industry where market access is better. The elasticity is estimated at −0.49, with a standard error of 0.207 (figure 5.7).[3] Improved market connectivity will increase profitability of the fishery industry and encourage more people to work in the sector.

FIGURE 5.7
Correlation between number of crews and market access

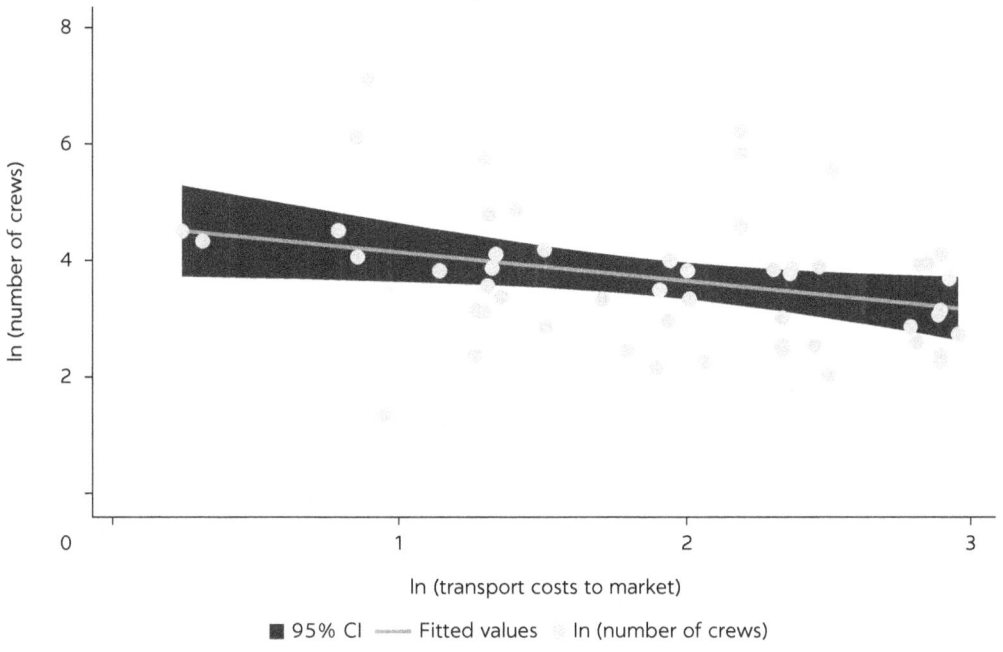

Source: World Bank estimate.

FIRM AGGLOMERATION

The formal industry and service sectors are thin in Liberia. According to a recent labor force survey, approximately 17,000 people are employed in the manufacturing sector and 343,000 in the service sector (table 5.2) (LISGIS 2011). Agriculture is an important sector, employing approximately half of the labor force. A significant number of people work in the informal sector, including agriculture, which accounts for nearly 60 percent of the total labor force.

The economic geography literature suggests that agglomeration economies can make an industrial cluster or a city attractive (Fujita et al. 1999; Krugman 1991). Despite the fact that the cost of distance has been declining in recent years because of new technologies, such as information and communications technology, firms still prefer to be located close to one another to share the common input markets of labor and intermediate inputs and thus minimize trade and transaction costs. The literature generally confirms this (Cieślik and Ryan 2004; Lee et al. 2012; Mare and Graham 2013; Milner et al. 2006; Procher 2011).

In Liberia, economic activities are highly concentrated in Monrovia, where more than 1.2 million people, or about one-quarter of the total population, live. The distribution of firm location is even more skewed (figure 5.8). According to the government's business registry database, more than 41,000 firms were officially registered in Liberia as of 2016 (table 5.3). Approximately 80 percent are located in Montserrado County, which includes Monrovia.

It is likely that transport connectivity and market accessibility play an important role in influencing firms' decisions on where to locate. There is a clear correlation between firm location and transport costs to market (map 5.3); more firms are located where market access is better.

TABLE 5.2 **Labor statistics in Liberia**

COUNTY	POPULATION	LABOR FORCE		INFORMAL EMPLOYMENT	
	(1,000)	(1,000)	% OF TOTAL	(1,000)	% OF LABOR FORCE
Bomi	101	31	30.7	20	64.5
Bong	379	179	47.2	108	60.3
Grand Bassa	201	75	37.3	51	68.0
Grand Cape Mount	120	62	51.7	39	62.9
Grand Gedeh	79	27	34.2	21	77.8
Grand Kru	54	26	48.1	16	61.5
Lofa	234	135	57.7	86	63.7
Margibi	219	75	34.2	41	54.7
Maryland	96	28	29.2	17	60.7
Montserrado	1,152	362	31.4	197	54.4
Nimba	427	164	38.4	77	47.0
Rivercess	70	35	50.0	20	57.1
Sinoe	90	18	20.0	9	50.0
River Gee	55	22	40.0	17	77.3
Gbarpolu	61	34	55.7	23	67.6
Total	3,338	1,273	38.1	742	58.3

Source: LISGIS 2011.

FIGURE 5.8
Geographic concentration in Liberia

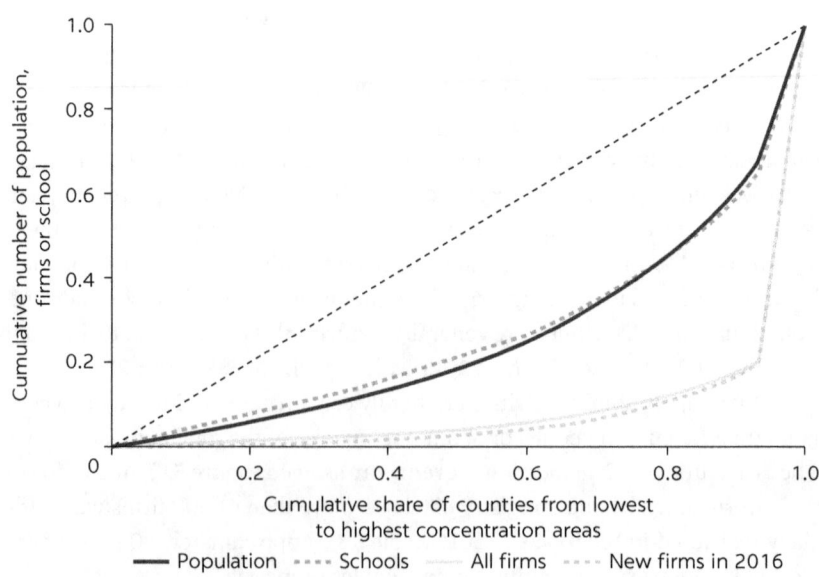

Source: World Bank estimate.

TABLE 5.3 **Firms registered, 2016**

COUNTY	NUMBER OF FIRMS	SHARE (%)
Bomi	258	0.6
Bong	1,090	2.6
Gbarpolu	149	0.4
Grand Bassa	1,063	2.6
Grand Cape Mount	289	0.7
Grand Gedeh	611	1.5
Grand Kru	74	0.2
Lofa	499	1.2
Margibi	1,849	4.4
Maryland	475	1.1
Montserrado	33,421	80.2
Nimba	1,255	3.0
River Gee	338	0.8
Rivercess	70	0.2
Sinoe	251	0.6
Total	41,692	100.0

Source: Liberia Business Registry Database.
Note: Percentages may not add up to 100 percent due to rounding.

MAP 5.3
Number of firms registered by district, 2016

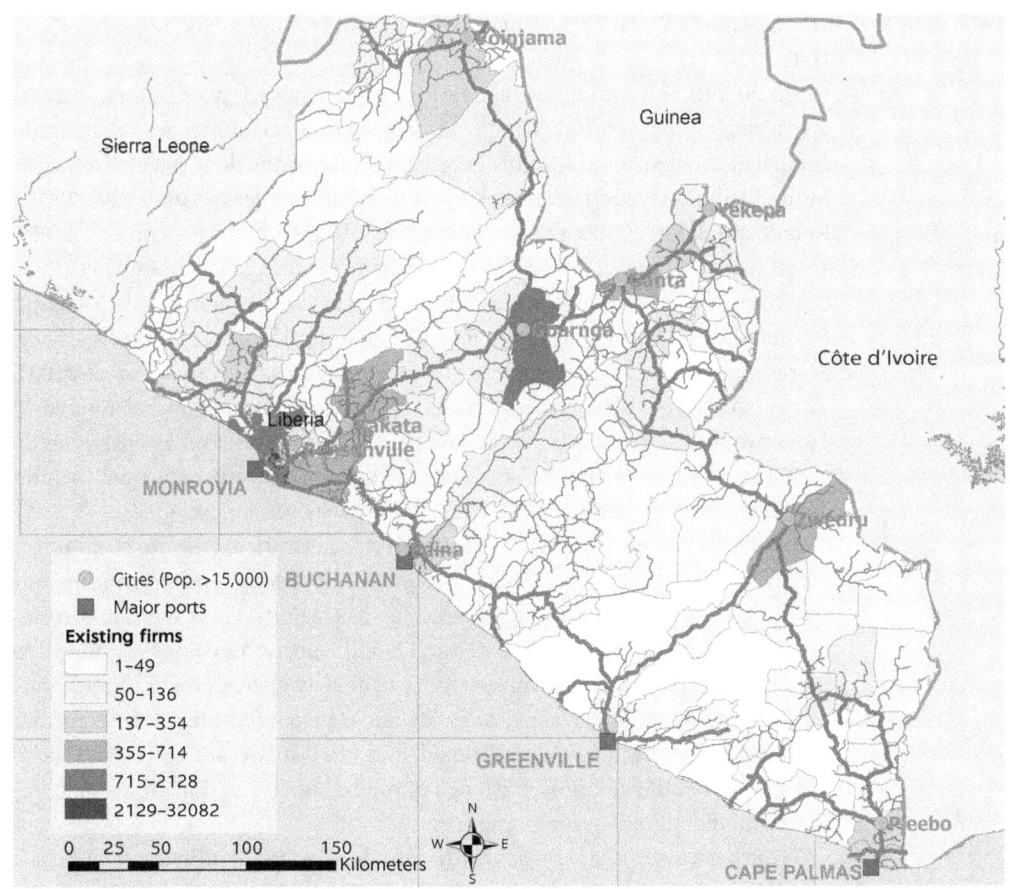

Source: Liberia Business Registry Database.

More formally, using firm registry data in Liberia, the instrumental variable spatial autoregressive model is applied to examine the effects of transport connectivity on firms' decisions on where to locate (Iimi and Rao 2018a). There are empirical challenges, such as spatial externalities and endogeneity of infrastructure development. There are significant spatial spillover effects and transport connectivity is endogenous. Firms are more likely to be located where road density is high and market access is greater.

The data also indicate strong agglomeration economies. Therefore, the primary city, Monrovia, is likely to continue growing and attracting more people and firms. Secondary cities can also grow with improved transport connectivity across populated areas, such as district centers. To stimulate agglomeration economies, transport connectivity needs to be improved between Monrovia and nonprimary cities such as Ganta and Harper where regional connectivity is also important.

SOCIAL BENEFITS: HEALTH CARE ACCESS

In general, health care access is a challenge in rural areas. The available literature shows that people who live in remote areas have limited access to good quality health services (Bourke et al. 2012; Gamm et al. 2003; Institute of Medicine 2005). Even in the United States, rural residents are less likely to visit the emergency department than their urban counterparts (Lishner et al. 2000). In the United States, approximately 20 percent of the total population lives in rural areas, but only 9 percent of physicians practice in rural areas (Rosenblatt and Hart 2000).

Limited rural health access can be attributed to a variety of factors. In rural areas, geographic conditions and transport service availability are unfavorable compared to urban areas (Klemick et al. 2009). Rural dwellers' travel distance to health facilities is much longer than that of urban dwellers (Gamm et al. 2003). Nemet and Bailey (2000) show that not only distance, but also people's activity space, including grocery shops and community centers, determines health care use. In rural areas, these facilities tend to be scattered or unavailable. Demand for health services may also be weak because rural residents are often poor. Subscription to health insurance is lower in rural areas (Jovanovic et al. 2003). The quality of health services may also be lower in rural areas because rural physicians often have to see more patients than urban doctors. Bronstein et al. (1997) show that rural health services are cheaper, but fewer episodes include outpatient facility charges, and fewer ancillary services are provided.

In Liberia, the coverage of the health service network appears to be comprehensive, with hospitals and clinics located evenly throughout the country, but transport connectivity varies significantly across regions. There is broad correlation between transport connectivity and health care access. Four variables are used to measure transport connectivity: road density, share of roads in good condition,[4] transport cost to reach a large city, and transport cost to reach Monrovia. The first two indicators are traditional, and the last two are newer and more complex, reflecting not only existence of roads, but also optimal route calculation to minimize vehicle operating costs.

Health care access increases with road density and quality and decreases with transport costs to a market or port. Health care access is measured according to the total number of patients who visited each health facility and

FIGURE 5.9
Health care access and transport connectivity

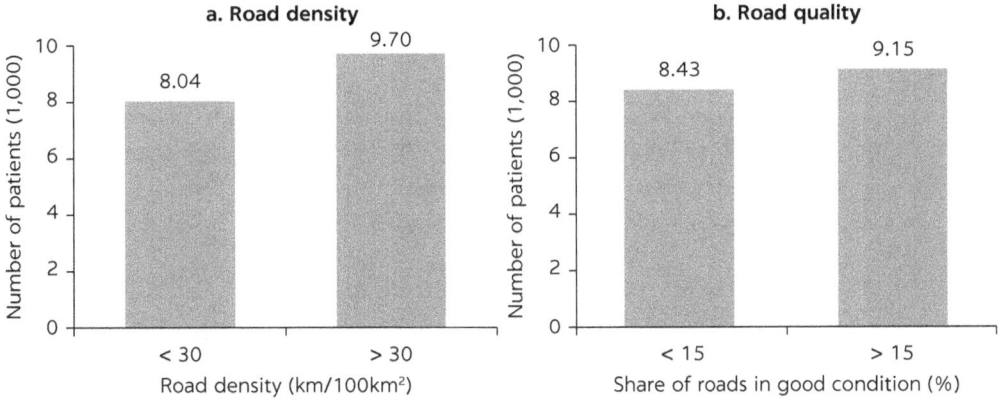

Source: World Bank estimate.

had a medical consultation at their outpatient department in 2015 (figure 5.9). The average number of outpatient departments is 8,000 at hospitals around which road density is less than 30 kilometers per 100 km^2 and 9,700 where road density is greater than 30 kilometers per 100 km^2. Many other factors are related to road infrastructure and health access. Causality is unclear. The number of patients seems to be slightly higher when the share of roads in good condition is greater.

More formally, with particular attention paid to the possible question of endogeneity associated with infrastructure investment, the instrumental variable technique is applied. Transport connectivity, especially higher road density, can increase health care access (Iimi and Rao 2018b), but it was found that road quality has no significant effect. In addition, the statistical effect of road density varies depending on distance from a health facility. The effect is particularly significant within a 30- to 50-kilometer radius. The analysis includes only hospitals and health centers for which facility level performance data are available. The result can be interpreted to mean that rural accessibility as well as broader transport connectivity need to be improved to promote people's access to a higher level of health care services.

POTENTIAL TRIP DELAY COSTS CAUSED BY ROAD FLOODING

As discussed above, Liberia is vulnerable to climate events and the road network is vulnerable to high rainfall and floods. Road flooding imposes a variety of costs on the economy, such as infrastructure damage, emergency response, travel time delay, disruption of transport mobility, more vehicle mileage associated with detour routes, and greater accident risk (Hallenbeck, Goodchild, and Drescher 2014). The potential cost of coastal floods to major port cities all over the world is estimated at US$3 trillion for a 100-year flood event (Hanson et al. 2011). It is estimated that floods cost on average US$5.4 million in the United States every year. Average traffic speed can fall by 10 to 25 percent, and average traffic volumes can decrease by 15 to 30 percent with flooding (U.S. Department of Transportation). A recent study on flood risk in the San Francisco Bay Area estimated that damage to structures would amount to a cost of US$5.9 billion. Travel time delays would range from 30 to 60 minutes, leading to a delay cost of US$78 million (Berkman and Brown 2015).

In Liberia, the climate resilience of different roads and structures may differ. For instance, the Monrovia-Ganta corridor, which is approximately 250 kilometers long, has just been rehabilitated, and new bridges have been designed with a 100-year design life, so normal precipitation is unlikely to cause major road closures, but most other roads are still susceptible to climate events. Many existing structures are in poor condition, and some necessary bridges and culverts may be missing.

The cost of travel delays was examined to determine the possible effect of floods. Actual effects should have been examined with a variety of issues taken into account, such as uncertainty regarding climate change, resilience of individual roads and structures, capacity of society to adapt, and importance of individual economic activities (difference in value of time between economic agents) (Hallenbeck, Goodchild, and Drescher 2014). The intensity of possible flood risk is different in different areas (map 5.4). For simplicity, a fragility curve was developed based on experimental data and actual vehicle operating data (Pregnolato, Ford, and Dawson 2015). There is a threshold for physical road passability at an approximate water depth of 300 mm (figure 5.10). For computational purposes, speed reduction is assumed to be nearly but not exactly 100 percent beyond this threshold.[5] The value of time is assumed to be US¢ 20 per ton-hour.[6]

MAP 5.4
Twenty-five-year flood depth

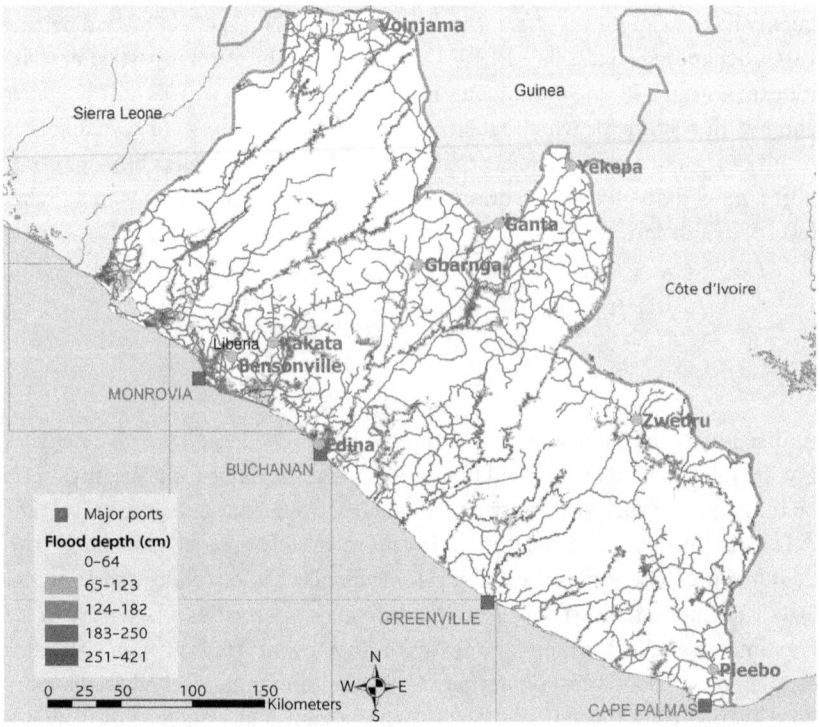

Source: United Nations International Strategy for Disaster Reduction Global Assessment Report database.

Based on these assumptions, it is estimated that a 25-year flood could increase transport costs by 8.2 percent on average. Compared to the normal case (figure 1.5), the difference may appear minimal (map 5.5), but the potential effects differ in different areas. Some places are more susceptible than others (map 5.6). In addition, the estimated costs are associated only with trip delays

FIGURE 5.10
Road fragility curve

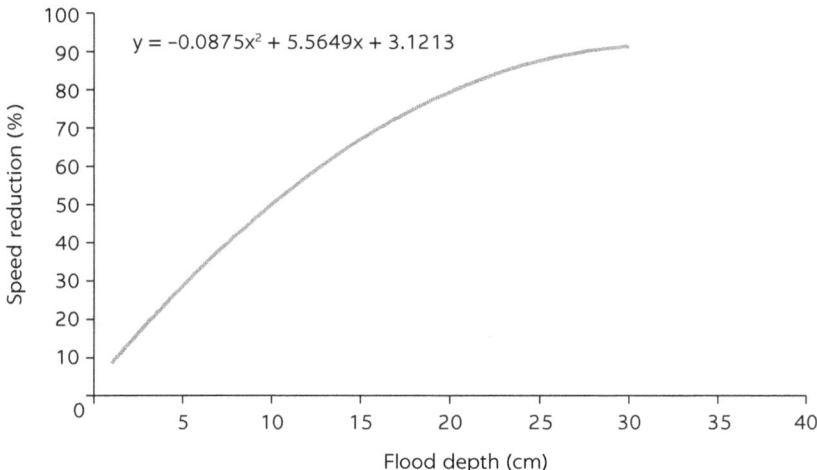

$y = -0.0875x^2 + 5.5649x + 3.1213$

Source: Based on Pregnolato, Ford, and Dawson 2015.

MAP 5.5
Transport costs to market under flood scenario

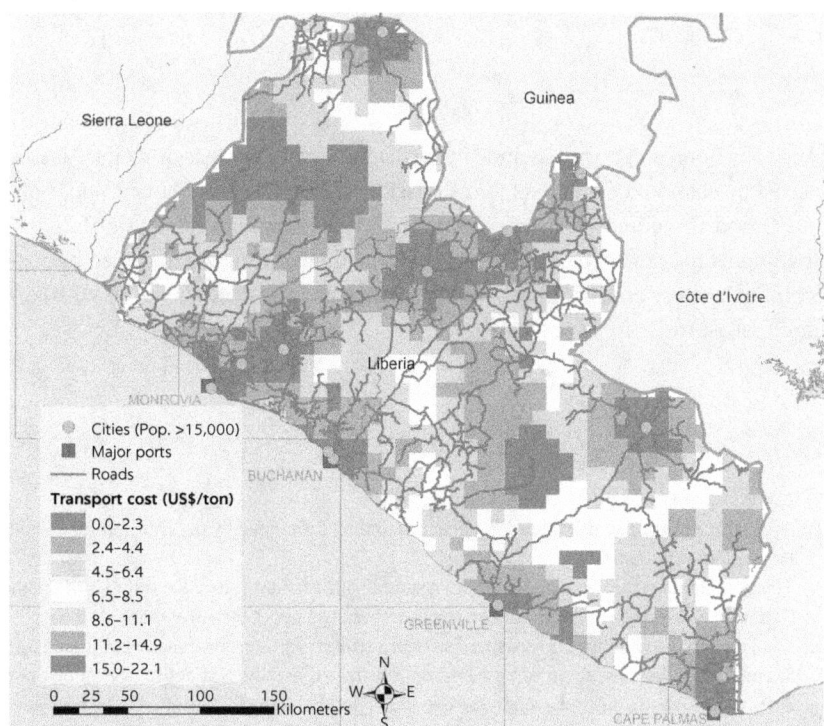

Source: World Bank estimate.

MAP 5.6
Change in transport costs caused by potential floods

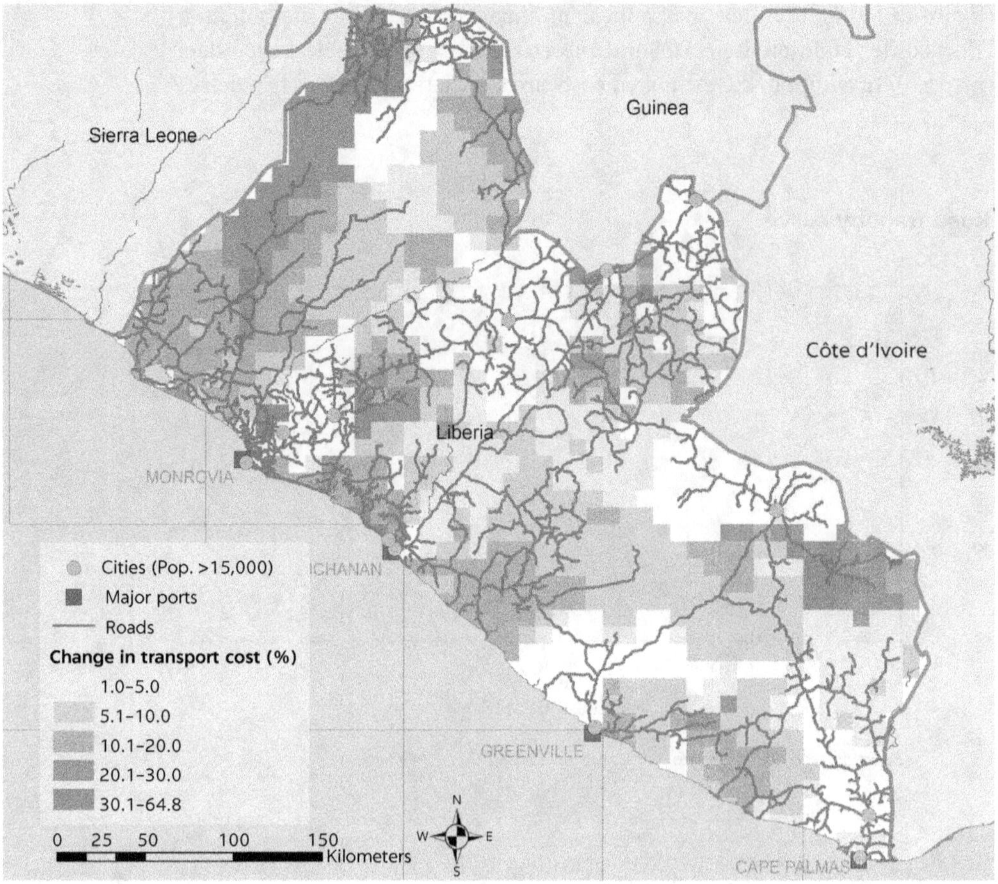

Source: World Bank estimate.

caused by flood and do not include infrastructure damage costs or welfare losses caused by abandoned trips. As far as possible travel delays are concerned, Lofa and Grand Gedeh counties are particularly vulnerable to heavy rainfall and flooding. Some peri-urban areas in Montserrado and Margibi may also be susceptible. In these areas, it may be worth examining the necessity of some adaptation measures.

NOTES

1. According to World Development Indicators.
2. According to the spatial production allocation model developed by the International Food Policy Research Institute.
3. The unit of analysis is landing site. With a sample of 54 landing sites, the number of crews (Liberian and foreign) is regressed on the estimated transport costs to a market.
4. Road density and quality are measured within a 10-km radius around each health facility.
5. Speed reduction is assumed to be 95 percent if the expected flood depth is greater than 300 mm, which means that even in the event of a flood, the road is assumed to be passable, albeit at a very slow speed. No trip would have been abandoned or diverted.

6. According to the U.S. Department of Transportation, the time value for truck is US$24.70 per hour. With a difference in GDP per capita between the United States and Liberia taken into account, the time value is assumed to be US$0.20 per hour. A 1-ton pickup truck is considered for simplicity.

REFERENCES

Bell, Clive, and Susanne van Dillen. 2012. "How Does India's Rural Roads Program Affect the Grassroots? Finding from a Survey in Orissa." World Bank Policy Research Working Paper 6167. World Bank, Washington, DC.

Berkman, Mark P., and Toby Brown. 2015. "Estimating Flood Impacts: A Status Report." Presented at the Australasian Coasts & Ports Conference. Auckland, New Zealand. 15–18 September, 2015.

Bronstein, J.M., V.A. Johnson, and C.A. Fargason Jr. 1997. How rural physicians compare on cost and quality measures for Medicaid ambulatory care episodes. *Journal of Rural Health*. Vol. 13(2), pp. 126–135.

Bourke, Lisa, John Humphreys, John Wakerman, and Judy Taylor. 2012. Understanding rural and remote health: A framework for analysis in Australia. *Health and Place*, Vol. 18, pp. 496–503.

Cieślik, Andrzej, and Michael Ryan. 2004. Explaining Japanese direct investment flows into an enlarged Europe: A comparison of gravity and economic potential approaches. *Journal of the Japanese and International Economies*, Vol. 8(1), pp. 12–37.

Dercon, Stefan, Daniel O. Gilligan, John Hoddinott, and Tassew Woldehanna. 2007. "The Impact of Roads and Agricultural Extension on Consumption Growth and Poverty in Fifteen Ethiopian Villages." CSAE WPS/2007-01. Oxford University, Oxford, United Kingdom.

Elbadawi, Ibrahim, Taye Mengistae, and Albert Zeufack. 2006. "Market Access, Supplier Access, and Africa's Manufactured Exports: An Analysis of the Role of Geography and Institutions." World Bank Policy Research Working Paper No. 3942. World Bank, Washington, DC.

Fujita, Masahisa, Paul Krugman, and Anthony Venables. 1999. *The Spatial Economy*. MIT Press.

Gamm, Larry, Graciela Castillo, and Stephanie Pittman. 2003. Access to quality health services in rural areas: Primary care: A literature review. In "Rural Healthy People 2010" edited by Larry Gamm, Linnae Hutchison, Betty Dabney, and Alicia Dorsey. Available at http://sph.tamhsc.edu/centers/rhp2010/publications.htm.

Global Integrity. 2011. *Global integrity Report 2011*. Available at https://www.globalintegrity.org/research/reports/global-integrity-report/global-integrity-report-2011/.

Hallenbeck, Mark, Anne Goodchild, and Jerome Drescher. 2014. "Travel Costs Associated with Flood Closures of State Highways Near Centralia/Chehalis, Washington." Washington State DoT Research Report WA-RD 832.1. Washington State Department of Transportation, Olympia, WA.

Hanson, Susan, Robert Nicholls, N. Ranger, S. Hallegatte, C. Corfee-Morlot, C. Herweijer, and J. Chateau. 2011. "A Global Ranking of Port Cities with High Exposure to Climate Extremes." *Climatic Change* 104: 89–111.

Holl, Adelheid. 2004. "Manufacturing Location and Impacts of Road Transport Infrastructure: Empirical Evidence from Spain." *Regional Science and Urban Economics* 34(3): 341–63.

Iimi, Atsushi, and Kulwinder Rao. 2018a. "Firm Location Transport Connectivity and Agglomeration Economies." World Bank Policy Research Working Paper 8411. World Bank, Washington, DC.

Iimi, Atsushi, and Kulwinder Rao. 2018b. "Transport connectivity and health care access: evidence from Liberia." World Bank Policy Research Working Paper 8413. World Bank, Washington, DC.

Institute of Medicine. 2005. "Quality Through Collaboration: The Future of Rural Health." Available at: http://www.iom.edu/Reports/2004/Quality-Through-Collaboration-The-Future-of-Rural-Health.aspx#sthash.nqB3dnEa.dpuf.

Jovanovic, Zorana, Chyongchiou Lin, and Chung-Chou Chang. 2003. Uninsured vs. insured population: variations among nonelderly Americans. *Journal of Health and Social Policy*, Vol. 17(3), pp. 71–85.

Khandker, Shahidur R., Zaid Bakht, and B. Gayatri Koolwal. 2009. "The Poverty Impact of Rural Roads: Evidence from Bangladesh." *Economic Development and Cultural Change* 57(4): 685–722.

Klemick, Heather, Kenneth Leonard, and Melkiory Masatu. 2009. Defining access to health care: Evidence on the importance of quality and distance in rural Tanzania. *American Journal of Agricultural Economics*, Vol. 91(2), pp. 347–58.

Krugman, Paul. 1991. Increasing returns and economic geography. *Journal of Political Economy*, Vol. 99(3), 483–499.

Kruk, Margaret E., Peter C. Rockers, Elizabeth H. Williams, S. Tornorlah Varpilah, Rose Macauley, Geetor Saydee, and Sandro Galea. 2010. "Availability of Essential Health Services in Post-Conflict Liberia." *Bulletin of the World Health Organization* 88: 527–34.

Lee, Ki-Dong, Seok-Joon Hwang, and Min-hwan Lee. 2012. Agglomeration economies and location choice of Korean manufactures within the United States. *Applied Economics*, Vol. 44, pp. 189–200.

Lall, Somik V. and Taye Mengistae. 2005. "The Impact of Business Environment and Economic Geography on Plant-Level Productivity: An Analysis of Indian Industry." World Bank Policy Research Working Paper No. 3664. World Bank, Washington, DC.

LISGIS (Liberia Institute of Statistics and Geo-Information Services). 2009. "Liberia: 2008 National Population and Housing Census Final Results." Liberia Institute of Statistics and Geo-Information Services, Monrovia, Liberia.

LISGIS. 2011. "Report on the Liberia Labour Force Survey 2010." Liberia Institute of Statistics and Geo-Information Services, Monrovia, Liberia.

LISGIS. 2017. Liberia Institute of Statistics & Geo-Information Services. (2017). Household Income and Expenditure Survey 2016 Statistical Abstract.

Lishner, Denise, Roger Rosenblatt, Laura-Mae Baldwin, and Gary Hart. 2000. Emergency department use by the rural elderly, *Journal of Emergency Medicine*, Vol. 18(3), pp. 289–297.

Limão, Nuno, and Anthony Venables. 2001. "Infrastructure, Geographical Disadvantage, Transport Costs, and Trade." *The World Bank Economic Review* 15(3): 451–79.

Mare, David, and Daniel Graham. 2013. Agglomeration elasticities and firm heterogeneity. *Journal of Urban Economics*, Vol. 75, pp. 44–56.

Medda, Francesca, and Lourdes Trujillo. 2010. Short-sea shipping: an analysis of its determinants. *Maritime Policy & Management*, Vol. 37(2), pp 285–303.

Milner, Chris, Geoff Reed, and Pawin Talerngsri. 2006. Vertical linkages and agglomeration effects in Japanese FDI in Thailand. *Journal of The Japanese and International Economies*, Vol. 20(2), pp. 193–208.

Ministry of Transport. 2012. "National Transport Master Plan." Ministry of Transport, Monrovia, Liberia.

Nemet, Gregory, and Adrian Bailey. 2000. Distance and health care utilization among the rural elderly. Social Science and Medicine, Vol. 50, pp. 1197–1208.

Pregnolato, Maria, Alistair Ford, and Richard Dawson. 2015. "Analysis of the Risk of Transport Infrastructure Disruption from Extreme Rainfall." Presented at the 2015 International Conference on Applications of Statistics and Probability in Civil Engineering, Vancouver, Canada. July 12–15, 2015.

Procher, Vivien. 2011. "Agglomeration Effects and the Location of FDI: Evidence from French First-Time Movers." *Annals of Regional Science* 46: 295–312

Roberts, Peter, K. C. Shyam, and Cordula Rastogi. 2006. "Rural Access Index: A Key Development Indicator." Transport Papers TP-10. The World Bank Group, Washington, DC.

Rosenblatt, Roger, and Gary Hart. 2000. Physicians and rural America, *Western Journal of Medicine*, Vol. 173(5), pp. 348–351.

Samimi, C., A.H. Fink, and H. Paeth. 2012. "The 2007 Flood in the Sahel: Causes, Characteristics and Its Presentation in the Media and FEWS NET." *Natural Hazards and Earth System Sciences* 12: 313–25.

TRB (Transportation Research Board). 2002, "Comparison of Inland Waterways and Surface Freight Modes," TR NEWS 221, Transportation Research Board (www.trb.org), July-August 2002.

UNCTAD (United Nations Conference on Trade and Development). (2015). *Review of Maritime Transport* 2015. New York: United Nations Conference on Trade and Development.

UN-Habitat (United Nations Human Settlements Programme). 2013. *State of the World's Cities: Prosperity of Cities 2012/2013*.

U.S. Department of Transportation, Federal Highway Administration. "How Do Weather Events Impact Roads?" Washington, DC: U.S. Department of Transportation.

Wilmsmeier, Gordon, Jan Hoffmann, and Ricardo J. Sanchez. 2006. "The Impact of Port Characteristics on International Maritime Transport Costs." *Research in Transportation Economics: Port Economics* 16: 117–40.

World Bank. 2016a. *Measuring Rural Access: Using New Technologies*. Washington, DC: World Bank.

World Bank. 2016b. *Making the Most of Ports in West Africa*. Forthcoming. Washington, DC: World Bank.

6 Financial Requirements and Further Works

TENTATIVE FINANCIAL REQUIREMENT ESTIMATES

Although precise estimation is out of the scope of the current report and difficult given available data, the above discussion clearly suggests that a wide range of connectivity needs remain to be met. This calls for strategic prioritization. This section aims to understand the approximate magnitude of the likely financial requirements, primarily focused on the road sector.[1] It should be interpreted as an indicative result: further works are needed to obtain more accurate estimates, as will be discussed below.

Important caveats are as follows: first, the estimation is based on the data that were obtained and analyzed as of 2016. Some of the identified needs may already have been addressed by ongoing projects or programs. These are not taken into account. Second, the estimation is focused on the need for road improvements. Other types of transport infrastructure, such as ports and railways, as well as non-transport complementary facilities, logistic infrastructure, and storage facilities also need to be improved. Due to data deficiency, however, these are left for future analysis. In addition, road structures are excluded from the estimation because the costs of road structures vary significantly across individual cases. Thus, the estimates should be interpreted as the minimum. Third, maintenance needs are not included, though absolutely critical. Finally, the calculation assumes simple average road rehabilitation costs of US$1 million for paved roads and US$75,000 for gravel roads.

Primary roads. Following the above discussion in the report, different types of interventions are considered (table 6.1). It is the first priority to keep improving and maintaining the primary road network, which is fundamental to ensuring the efficient mobility of goods and people across the country. The majority of paved roads have already been rehabilitated. About 2,200 km of unpaved roads are assumed to in need of an upgrade, which would cost US$2,152 million.

Rural access. In addition, US$1,203 million would be needed to achieve universal rural access. As discussed above, US$850 million would be required to rehabilitate the country's current road network. Excluding the primary network,

TABLE 6.1 **Tentative estimates of financial requirements**

OBJECTIVES/INTERVENTIONS	DESCRIPTION/ASSUMPTIONS	FINANCIAL NEEDS (US$ MILLIONS)
1. Primary road network		**2,230**
Rehabilitate paved primary roads	About 490 km of paved roads are in good condition, but about 80 km of paved roads are in fair to poor condition. These roads are assumed to be rehabilitated	78
Upgrade unpaved primary roads	About 2,200 km of unpaved primary roads are in fair to poor condition. These roads are assumed to be upgraded	2,152
2. Universal rural access		**1,203**
Rehabilitate the current road network	All classified roads are assumed to need to be in good condition. Exclusive of the above, about 8,100 km of non-primary roads will be rehabilitated. Still, RAI would be 73%	606
Construct (or reclassify) new rural roads	To achieve universal access, at least about 8,000 km of additional rural roads would be needed given the current population density along typical rural roads	597
Total		**3,433**

Source: World Bank estimate.
Note: RAI = Rural access index.

about US$606 million would be needed. This is not enough to achieve universal access. Some people live beyond the current road network.[2] To provide access to them, it is estimated that about 8,000 km of roads need to be constructed or classified from the currently unclassified roads. Assuming these roads are in poor condition, rehabilitation would cost US$597 million.

Total requirements. All possible road improvement works are covered by one of these two interventions for the primary road network and universal rural access. Therefore, the total financial requirement is estimated at US$3,433 million in the road sector. As mentioned, this should be considered as the minimum. Additional resources should be required for road structures as well as periodic and routine road maintenance.

Different development objectives could be pursued at different costs (table 6.2). These are not a complete list, but examined for illustration purposes. Further detailed assessments are needed to more accurately estimate financial requirements.

Agricultural roads. To promote agricultural production, it is estimated that US$333 million would be needed to connect major production areas to domestic markets. Based on the SPAM data, there are about 8,000 km^2 of land that produce about half of Liberia's total crop production (map 6.1). This may represent about 15 percent of the current agricultural land. To connect these areas to domestic market defined by towns with a population of more than 15,000, 1,050 km of roads need to be improved. Most of these roads are currently unpaved. About US$108 million would be required.

An additional US$225 million may be needed to provide better market access for more rural people. It is assumed that half of the major crop production areas (according to the total production value estimate at each location) would be connected. The threshold for this target is estimated at US$330,000 per 100 km^2 or US$33 per ha. About 3,200 km of feeder roads need to be rehabilitated.

TABLE 6.2 **Estimated financial requirements by development areas**

OBJECTIVES/ INTERVENTIONS	DESCRIPTION/ASSUMPTIONS	FINANCIAL NEEDS (US$ MILLIONS)
A. Promote major agricultural production		**333**
Connect top 15% major production areas to markets	To connect key production areas (producing US$1 million per 100 km^2) to domestic markets, about 1,050 km of roads need to be improved, out of which 31 km are currently paved roads	108
Connect half of crop production areas to markets	To connect other minor production areas (producing US$330,000 to US$1 million per 100 km^2) to domestic markets, an additional 3,200 km of roads need to be improved, out of which 167 km are currently paved roads	225
B. Promote fishery production		**101**
Connect landing sites to domestic markets	To connect 90 landing sites to domestic markets, 1,250 km of roads are needed. Given the current road condition, 990 km of roads remain to be improved, out of which 29 km are currently paved roads	101
C. Improve health access		**331**
Connect major hospitals to Monrovia	To connect 90 hospitals and health centers to Monrovia, about 2,700 km of roads are needed. Given the current road condition, 2,080 km of roads remain to be improved, out of which 54 km are currently paved roads	207
Connect district centers to major hospitals	Additionally, to ensure connectivity between district centers and hospitals/health centers, about 1,730 km of roads are needed, out of which 1,630 km need to be improved	124
D. Improve connectivity among coastal cities		**At least 133**
Expand the capacity of Freeport of Monrovia	Freeport is becoming congested. Further analysis is needed to examine the feasibility and costs to use the rail line for other purposes	—
Develop cabotage between Monrovia and other ports	Further analysis is needed to examine the feasibility and costs to use the rail line for other purposes	—
Improve inland road connectivity from three ports (Buchanan, Greenville, and Harper)	To provide good port access to at least 200,000 people from each port, about 1,750 km of roads need to be improved. Almost all roads are currently unpaved	133
E. Improve rail connectivity between hinterland and Buchanan		**—**
Introduce non-mining freight operations to Lamco rail line	The Lamco rail line is operational under the mining concession agreement. Further analysis is needed to examine the feasibility and costs to use the rail line for other purposes	—
F. Promote regional connectivity by road		**At least 112**
Rehabilitate main regional corridors	The identified key regional corridor roads comprise 380 km of paved roads and 990 km of unpaved roads, out of which 41 km of paved and 950 km of unpaved roads need to be improved	112
Improve border crossing facilities and arrangements	It is important to improve not only regional roads, but also border crossings. Further analysis is needed to examine what would be needed on the physical and institutional sides	—
G. Strengthen climate resilience		**103–1,155**
Rehabilitate or upgrade roads that are located in flood-prone areas and in poor condition	About 1,350 km of roads are situated on flood-prone areas, out of which 1,150 km are not in good condition. It is assumed that these roads are either rehabilitated based on the current specifications or all upgraded. Further detailed analysis is needed	103–1,155

Source: World Bank estimate based on data provided by the government of Liberia.
Note: — denotes that the information is unavailable as of publication date.

MAP 6.1
Key areas to promote crop production

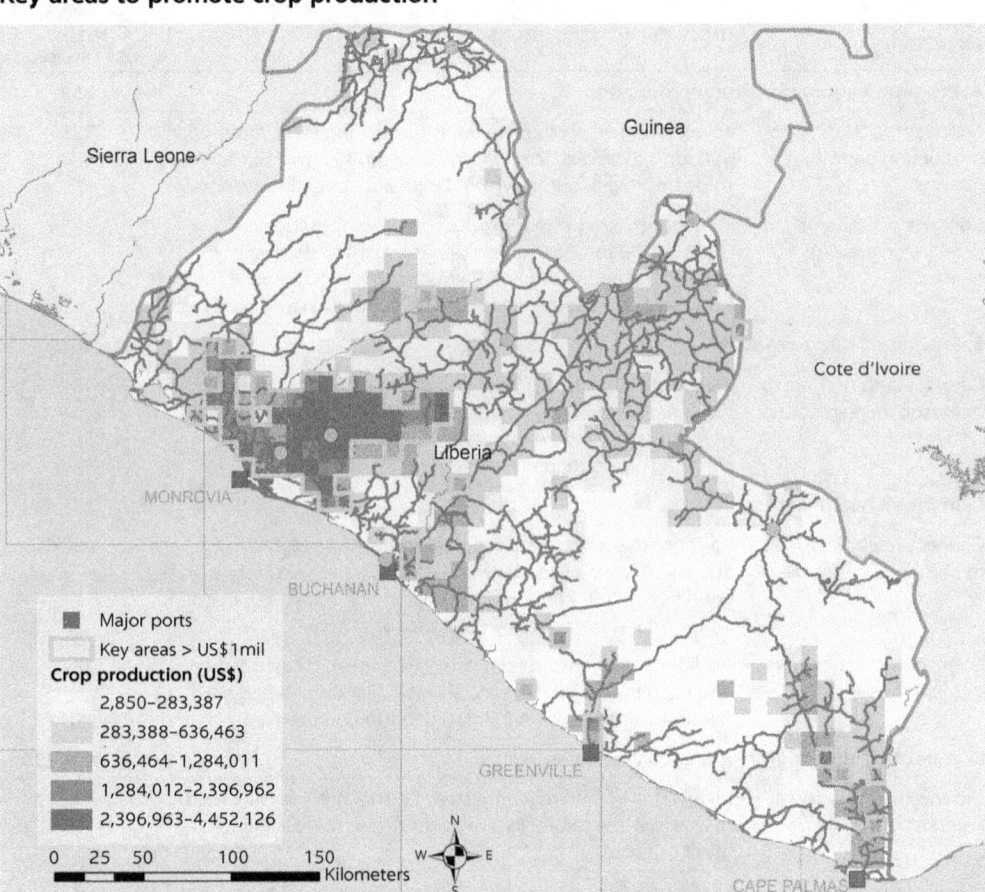

Source: World Bank estimate.

Fishery feeder roads. As discussed above, a different type of connectivity may be needed to promote the fishery industry. About US$100 million would be required to connect about 90 landing sites, which can be clustered into 55 areas, to domestic markets.

Health access. From the health access point of view, about US$330 million would be needed to connect major health facilities to Monrovia and then connect district centers to them. Specifically, significant resources are needed to connect health facilities to Monrovia mainly by the primary road network. This will cost US$207 million. Rural health care connectivity would also require some US$120 million.

Connectivity among coastal cities. Further analysis is needed to examine whether cabotage is feasible and how much would be needed. From the road infrastructure point of view, it would be important to improve inland road connectivity and ensure that there would be sufficient demand for each of the non-primary ports: Buchanan, Greenville, and Harper. It is assumed that local connectivity is ensured to cover at least 200,000 people from each port (map 6.2). Based on the current population distribution and road condition, different inland connectivity is assumed. While Buchanan needs a narrower market area because of high population density, Greenville would require a wider market area because of low population density as well as the currently poor condition of inland roads. To this end, at least US$133 million would be required.

MAP 6.2
Port hinterland to be connected to cover at least 200,000 people

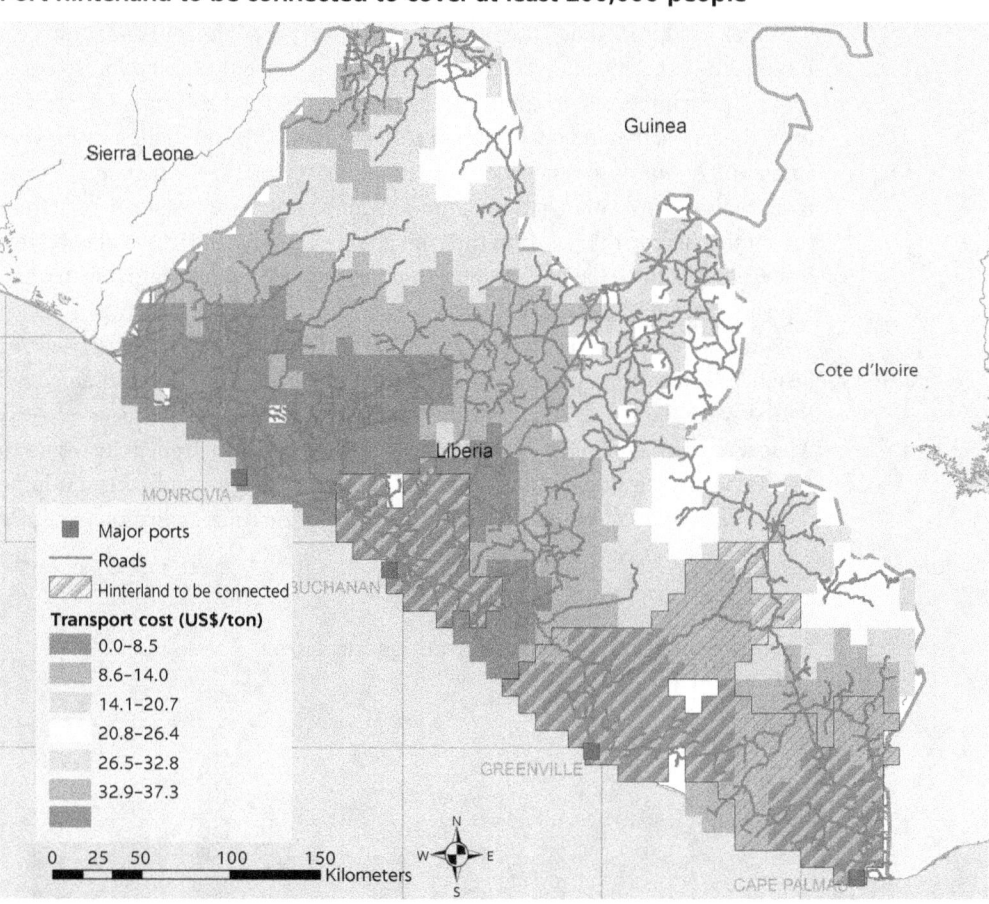

Source: World Bank estimate.

Regional connectivity. As discussed, about 1,400 km of roads are identified as possible regional corridors to connect border points and Monrovia. Except for paved roads, many unpaved roads remain to be improved. This would require US$112 million based on our assumed cost estimates. In addition, border facilities may need to be rehabilitated and institutional arrangements may also be improved at border crossings. Further detailed assessments are needed.

Climate resilience. There are about 1,350 km of roads that are in flood-prone areas and currently in poor condition. These are considered to be particularly vulnerable to possible extreme climate events. To rehabilitate them, at least US$103 million is needed. If they are assumed to be upgraded, it would cost US$1,155 million. There are other resilience technologies that can be applied using more bridges and culverts. The actual costs depend on which technologies are used.

POSSIBLE PARTNERSHIP WITH CONCESSIONAIRES FOR ROAD INVESTMENT AND MAINTENANCE

As discussed above, a significant amount of resources—probably more than US$3.4 billion—are required to rehabilitate and maintain the existing road network in Liberia. In general, road infrastructure can be financed by taxpayers or road users (i.e., toll fees, fuel levy, and other vehicle-related charges). The fiscal capacity of the government of Liberia is limited and is likely continue to be so. On the other hand, concessionaires are one of the heavy road users in the country. In Liberia, the extractive industry, including mining, agriculture, and forestry sectors, plays an important role in the economy. The reported government revenues from the extractive industry amount to more than US$100 million every year (figure 6.1). This accounts for 6–10 percent of GDP or 40–50 percent of gross fixed capital formulation in the country. About half of these revenues come from the mining sector, oil, gas, iron ore, and gold (table 6.3). Agricultural revenues from rubber and oil palm plantation amount to US$15 million, and forestry and timber generate US$12 million per year.

Some concessionaires invest in transport infrastructure by themselves. For instance, a large iron ore concessionaire, ArcelorMittal, operates the Lamco rail line between Buchanan and northern Nimba County, where it produces iron ore. A short rail connection (76 kilometers), Bong Mine Railway, from Bong Mines to Monrovia, is operated by China-Union Investment, the second-largest mining company in Liberia. In the road sector, however, the roles and responsibilities

FIGURE 6.1
Government revenues from extractive industry

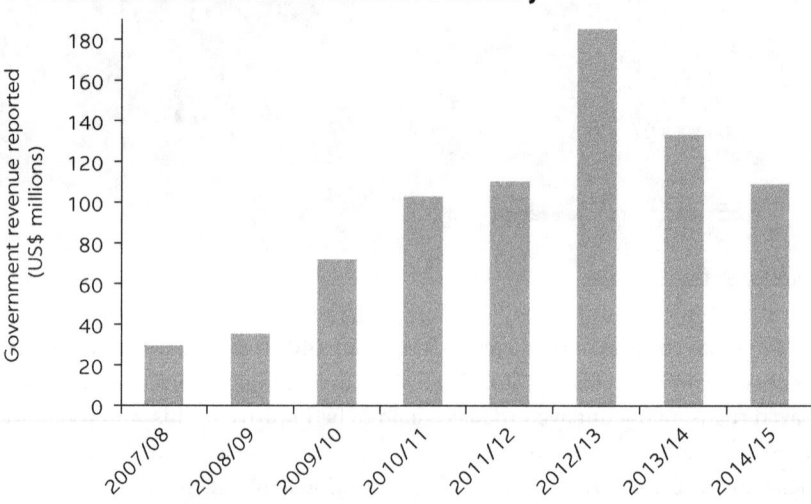

Source: Liberia EITI Report 2016.

TABLE 6.3 **Government revenues from extractive industry by sector, 2014/15**

SECTOR	GOVERNMENT REVENUES	
	US$ MILLION	% OF TOTAL
Mining	53.4	49.0
Of which, oil and gas	21.0	19.3
Agriculture	14.8	13.6
Forestry	11.5	10.6
Corp. social responsibility	8.3	7.6
Total	109.0	100.1

Source: Liberia EITI Report 2016.
Note: Percent may be more than 100% due to rounding.

TABLE 6.4 **Concession areas and road length by sector**

	CONCESSION AREAS		ROADS IN CONCESSION AREAS		
	AREA (KM²)	% OF TOTAL LAND	KM	% OF TOTAL NETWORK	KM NOT IN GOOD CONDITION
Mineral concessions	20,283	21.1	2,180	19.1	1,983
Timber sale contracts	204	0.2	31	0.3	27
Forest concessions	10,073	10.5	555	4.9	502
Agricultural concessions	4,425	4.6	516	4.5	438
Agro-forestry plantations	1,775	1.8	617	5.4	512

Source: World Bank estimate based on concession data from the Ministry of Lands, Mines and Energy.

may remain unclear between concessionaires and the government. While concessionaires presumably maintain access roads that are needed to export or transport outputs to their respective destinations, they have little incentive to develop or maintain other roads. From the road network point of view, fragmented road investment may not have achieved optimal connectivity for local residents.

An integrated systematic approach is needed to govern the roles and responsibilities for road development between concessionaires and the government. In Liberia, nearly 40 percent of land area is devoted to mining, agricultural, and forestry concessions (table 6.4). Mining concessionaires are currently granted as much as 21 percent of the total land. While agricultural concessions exist mainly in the northwestern region, agricultural plantations that produce rubber and oil palm are located in Margibi, Grand Bassa, and Maryland Counties. Forestry concession areas are currently concentrated in the southeastern region (map 6.3).[3]

There is an important opportunity for the government to partner with concessionaires to develop local connectivity. In these concession areas, there are about 3,900 km of roads, which account for approximately one-third of the total road network. According to the latest road condition survey, about 88 percent of roads in concession areas are not in good condition. If it is the responsibility of concessionaires to rehabilitate or maintain these roads, there must be a flaw in the regulatory or enforcement mechanism. If it is the responsibility of the government, the government may be able to strengthen partnership with concessionaires under certain arrangements. The active concessionaires in the country are generally profitable and have certain experience, though not specialized, to invest in road infrastructure. Under a proper agreement, they could implement one-third of the total road investment required. Further assessment is needed to decide whether and how to share the responsibilities and costs between the government and the private sector.

Liberia currently has an emerging experience in engaging the private sector for the development of various infrastructure projects, which has contributed to the economic development of the nation. The concessions in Liberia fall into four core sectors: mining, agriculture, forestry, and energy (table 6.5). As in 2014, forestry is the largest concession sector in Liberia (figure 6.2). From 2014 to 2016, economic activities in Liberia were severely affected by the Ebola crisis. Many infrastructure development efforts involving contracts and concessions were either suspended or became vulnerable to economic changes. After the crisis, concession-based activities have started to come back. Eight concession

MAP 6.3

Mining, agriculture, and forestry concession areas

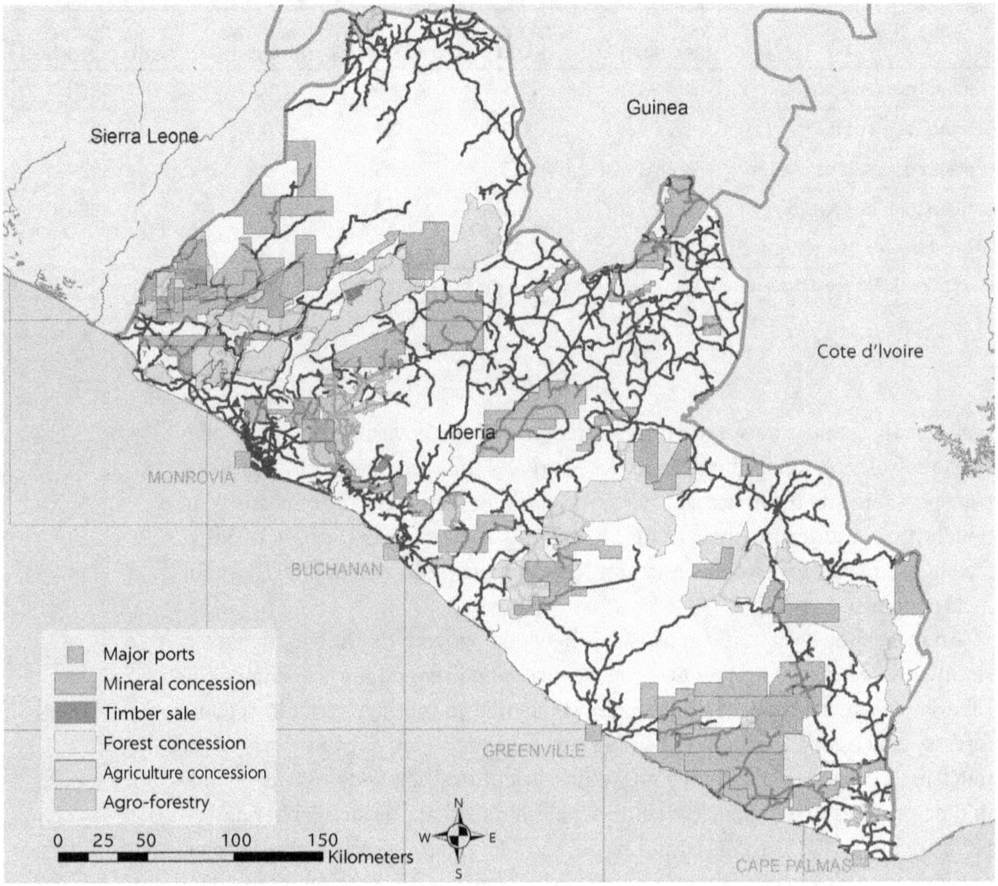

Source: Ministry of Lands, Mines and Energy.

TABLE 6.5 **Major concessions by sector**

SECTOR	MAJOR CONCESSIONAIRES
Mining	Western Cluster, ArcelorMittal, China-Union Investment, Putu Iron Ore, Bea Mountain Mining Corporation
Agriculture	Firestone Liberia, Liberia Agricultural Company, Golden Veroleum Liberia, Cavalla Rubber Corporation, Maryland Oil Palm Plantation
Forestry	Atlantic Resources, Akewa Group of Companies, Liberia Tree and Trading Company, Ecowood Inc., Bassa Timber and Logging, Sue Yeun
Energy	Oranto Petroleum, Woodside West Africa, Anadarko Liberia, CNOOC International Limited, Repsol Exploration

Source: National Bureau of Concessions.

activities were approved based on the PPC Act by the Public Procurement Concession Commission (PPCC) in 2016/17 (table 6.6).

The framework of concession agreements varies across sectors (table 6.7). The bidding parameter for most of the procurements in different sectors requires the bidder to quote a land lease rental in lieu of the development right over the land. A majority of the concessions require an upfront payment and surface rental fee as concession fee from the concessionaire. The average

FIGURE 6.2
Share of concessions, 2014

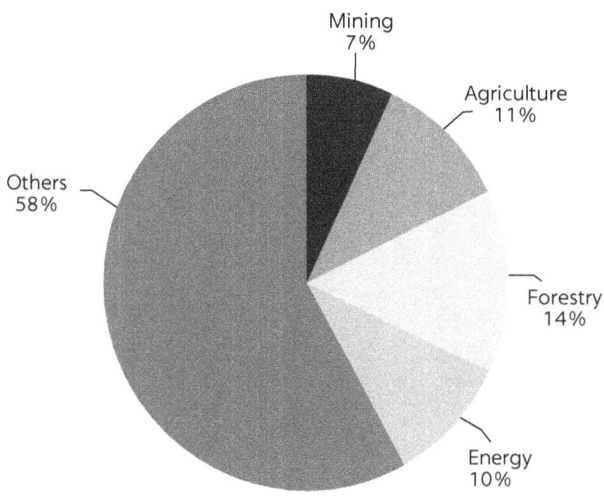

Source: National Bureau of Concessions.

TABLE 6.6 **Recent concession activities approved by PPCC**

SECTOR	DESCRIPTION OF CONCESSION	CONCESSION ENTITY
Infrastructure and Transport	Roberts International Airport Cargo Facility Construction	Liberia Airport Authority
	Development of the Port of Greenville	National Port Authority of Liberia
Energy and Infrastructure	Ten-Megawatt Electricity Generator (Renewable Energy)	Ministry of Lands, Mines and Energy
	Cross-Border Electrification (Grand Gedeh and Maryland)	Ministry of Lands, Mines and Energy
Commerce and Trade	Single-Window	Liberia Revenue Authority
	Electronic Fiscal Device	Liberia Revenue Authority
	Destination Inspection	Liberia Revenue Authority
	Verification of Conformity	Ministry of Commerce and Industry

Source: Public Procurement Concession Commission.

TABLE 6.7 **Basic characteristics of concession frameworks by sector**

	MINING	AGRICULTURE	FORESTRY	ENERGY
Area distribution	3,917.17 km^2	676,049 ha.	898,086 ha.	—
Duration	25 years	30–65 years	3–25 years	20–25 years
Average capital investment (approx.)	US$14m	US$22m	US$3m	US$0.2 M
Fiscal regime	Revenue Code (701–739)	Code (600–699)	As per FDA regulations	Code (740–799)
Tax (% on taxable income)	30%	Rice products: 10%	25%	30%
		Others: 25%		—

continued

TABLE 6.7, continued

	MINING	AGRICULTURE	FORESTRY				ENERGY
Other fees	Royalty:		Export fees (%):				Royalty: 10% on gross production
	Iron Ore: 4.5%		Type of tree				Signature Fees/Signing Bonus
	Gold and other metals: 3%		Type of products	Category A	B	C	These are bonuses or fees paid by extractive Industries to the government of Liberia for the signing of Concession Agreements.
	Commercial diamonds: 5%		Log	10	5	2.5	
			Wood	5	2.5	1.5	
Surface rental (US$ per acre)	Land within a mineral exploration license area: US$0.20	Developed land: US$2.00	Forest management contract: US$2.50				
		Undeveloped land: US$1.00	Timber sale Contract: US$1.25				
			Stumpage fee (%):				Paid to NOCAL as per square m of the area and the amount is stated in the Production Sharing Contract (PSC).
			Category A	B		C	
	Land within mining license area:		10	5		2.5	
	Year 1–10: US$5.00		Sawmill permit fee (US$)				
	Year 11–25: US$10.00		< 750m³	750–1,500m³		> 1,500m³	
			US$750	US$1,000		US$2,500	

Source: World Bank based on data provided by the government of Liberia.
Note: — denotes information is not available at time of publication.

investment requirements are high in the agriculture industry, with an average of US$22 million, followed by the mining industry (US$14 million). The duration for contracts and concessions in Liberia ranges between 3 and 65 years depending on the relevant industry and scope of work.

The general legal framework for public procurement in Liberia is robust and complies with most of the international best practices considering its relevance to both the Public Expenditure and Financial Accountability (PEFA) Performance Measurement Framework with Global Integrity's (GI) indicators used as benchmarks to evaluate transparency, fairness, and conflicts of interest to safeguard government procurement in 2011 (Global Integrity 2011[b]). The legal framework that governs concessions is guided by three key mechanisms: National Bureau of Concessions Act, Public Procurement & Concessions Commission (PPCC) Act, and Extractive Industries Transparency Initiative (EITI). See appendix B for detailed discussion.

Currently, the vulnerability of the transport infrastructure in the country has been dealt with by the concessionaires in different ways. Some concessionaires have directly developed their own port, rail, and energy infrastructure, while others also operate significant portions of the rural road network. In recent years, infrastructure development provisions for rehabilitation or creation of new infrastructure have been incorporated into natural resource concession contracts. For example, China-Union Investment has an obligation to rehabilitate infrastructure at Freeport of Monrovia, and ArcelorMittal has an obligation to rehabilitate the Port of Buchanan. China-Union Investment and ArcelorMittal also have an obligation to rehabilitate existing mining railway connected to their respective locations. There are three existing railways for use by the mining concessionaires: Buchanan to Yekepa, associated with ArcelorMittal (250 km); Monrovia to Bong Mines, associated with China-Union Investment (80 km); and Monrovia, via Tubmanburg, to Mano River at the border with Sierra Leone, associated with the Western Cluster Limited (145 km). All three are single-track systems.

A few concessionaires have been granted a right to construct with respect to the operation requirements in compliance with the contract with prior government approval. BHP Billiton, Putu Iron Ore, and Golden Veroleum Liberia have explicit rights to construct new ports in their concessions. They have also been given the right to construct new roads and railroads, with prior government approval, for the requirements of their operations.

Third-party access to concession infrastructure is required to be granted as long as spare capacity exists. This is the case for ports and railways. This provision has been the strongest in case of Putu Iron Ore Concession. The third-party access is granted as long as there is no interference with existing operations and associated costs are covered by third parties.

On the other hand, right to public infrastructure, such as public roads, is normally assured for concessionaires. No obligation to pay for repair or maintenance of such roads is imposed unless they are the sole user. However, there are cases where part of additional payment obligations are included and can be used to develop transport infrastructure in local areas. For example, the Maryland Oil Palm Plantation Concession signed on August 2, 2011, has provisions requiring the concessionaire to contribute US$5 per hectare annually to the community development fund and 1 percent of its annual gross sales of oil palm-related products to the oil palm development fund, to support local development in the development areas (also see appendix B for several case studies).

Therefore, there is potential to develop transport infrastructure in partnership with the private sector in Liberia. Currently, however, infrastructure provisions, though treated, are not done in a systematic or consistent manner, resulting in fragmented transport infrastructure developments and deficiency in the overall regional connectivity.

It is important to reduce and share the risks explicitly between the concessionaires and the government. From the private sector's point of view, there remain enormous risks in Liberia, a post-conflict country. Concessionaires already bear a significant part of the risks related to construction, design, operation and maintenance (availability), and financing of the public-private partnership projects. While the concession agreement covers all the major provisions for enhancing its own development, it is also imperative to further develop provisions for access and intermodal connectivity with road and rail transport with the government's support to seek optimal utilization of resources by both the government and the concessionaire.

At the same time, while there is a provision that the concessionaires have the right or obligation to improve their own or public infrastructure, it needs to further be stated that upon completion, it shall become public property. It is imperative that the policies to award concessions with infrastructure provisions to the private developers should be considered within the National Transportation Policy of Liberia. It also stated that third-party use may be granted as long as there is excess capacity and the technical and commercial terms of such benefits can be mutually agreed on between the government and the concessionaire, which would also protect the interest of the concessionaires.

FUTURE WORKS

The current report is focused on (a) compiling available spatial data, (b) visualizing current transport connectivity, (c) analyzing the relationship between transport connectivity and economic outcomes in the selected areas, and (d) providing a tentative list of priority areas and required financial resources. Notably, however, the report remains far from complete. Further detailed analyses are needed, including, but not limited to, the following:

Data gaps. There are still gaps in available data. For instance, few data are available for regional connectivity; actual fishery production data are not available; and agricultural data used in the report are only estimates based on the global crop production dataset. All these data should ideally be collected and updated.

Further development of a prioritization mechanism. Although the current work provided some tentative estimates of financial requirements for different development objectives, further discussion is needed to develop an actual prioritization mechanism. Some of the roads identified for different development objectives may overlap or compete with each other. A multi-criteria analysis can be used where certain weights are put to different objectives. Possible criteria include poverty incidence, rural accessibility, agricultural benefits, access to fishery landing sites, health care access, and network connectivity.

Detailed assessment of feasibility of road works. Once priority areas and/or clusters of roads are identified, further detailed assessment will be needed to determine technical, economic, and financial feasibility of particular road investments. In addition to social and environmental issues, contractual efficiency as well as implementation capacity should be taken into account.

Further assessment of institutional and complementary issues. Physical interventions must be supported by proper institutional frameworks and other complementary investments and reforms. For example, the current report does not provide detailed assessment on railway and port operations. For rural access, rural roads may not be sufficient to promote agricultural growth. Other investment may be needed in irrigation or logistics. For regional integration, regional roads are not sufficient. Regional trade arrangements must also be reviewed and improved, if needed.

Refinement of the whole prioritization framework. Taking all the above into account, a more complete and comprehensive prioritization and reform strategy needs to be developed as a continuous process over the medium to long term.

Review of possible financing arrangements between the government and concessionaires. Mining, agricultural, and forestry concessionaires are important economic players in Liberia. One-third of roads are located in their concession areas. A systematic approach is needed to define and share the responsibilities for road development between the government and concessionaires. To this end, a detailed review of the current arrangements is needed.

Currently, the government is preparing a national transport master plan for which the current report, hopefully, provides a lot of useful insights and views.

NOTES

1. Currently, a national transport master plan is under preparation. It will have a more comprehensive discussion across transport subsectors.
2. The 2-km road network coverage is considered following the definition of RAI.
3. Only existing concessionaires are taken into account. There are many other concession areas that are proposed or under preparation. The figure depicts only the concessions that are active, ratified, and identified according to the government data.

REFERENCE

Global Integrity. 2011. *Global Integrity Report 2011*. https://www.globalintegrity.org/research/reports/global-integrity-report/global-integrity-report-2011/.

7 Conclusion

Liberia is expected to recover from the Ebola crisis. Among other factors, limited transport connectivity is a significant challenge in the country. Fiscal resources are likely to continue to be limited, so strategic planning and allocation of public investment is essential.

To understand the needs correctly and prioritize transport investments, detailed and accurate data on road network and condition are critical. There were no detailed georeferenced road data in Liberia before this study. The first-ever detailed road inventory survey was conducted in 2016 and also covered road structures such as bridges and culverts. For planning and monitoring purposes, it is important for the government to continue such efforts toward updating the datasets periodically as part of road asset management systems.

The road inventory survey shows that there are 11,423 kilometers of roads in Liberia and approximately 2,900 bridges and 7,600 culverts. The survey revealed that current road network coverage is sufficient to provide transport mobility all over the country, although road quality remains a challenge except for a few major primary roads. Only 734 kilometers are currently paved, most of which are well maintained. The maintenance of the paved road network must be a priority from the network point of view. Approximately 60 percent of unpaved roads are in poor or very poor condition, which poses a significant challenge.

Connectivity is generally good around Monrovia and along the Monrovia-Ganta corridor, which has recently been rehabilitated. Based on transport costs, market and port accessibility are good in these areas. The vast majority of port traffic is through Freeport of Monrovia; due to the generally poor condition of the road network, accessibility is limited elsewhere. Rural accessibility is estimated at 41.9 percent and the mobility of the 2.3 million rural people unconnected to a good road network is significantly constrained. Inland road connectivity between the north and south is also limited. Lofa County and the southeastern regions have poor market accessibility and are completely disconnected from Monrovia, the largest market in the country, where one-quarter of the total population lives. Due to limited inland road connectivity, regional trade is minimal across inland borders.

Strategic prioritization is required given the wide range of these connectivity needs. Although further detailed assessments will be needed, it is tentatively estimated that the road sector would need at least US$3,433 million to maintain the primary road network and provide universal rural access. Additional resources should be required for road structures as well as periodic and routine road maintenance. By sector, the agricultural sector, including crop and fishery production, would likely to require the largest amount of resources, followed by the health sector. To provide better market access to half of the main crop production areas, US$333 million may be needed. Another US$100 million would be needed to connect fishery landing sites. Although many overlap with agricultural needs, it is estimated that US$330 million would be needed to ensure health care access in the country.

For other types of connectivity, tentative resource requirements are estimated but remain to be refined with missing data collected and other institutional issues examined further. More discussion is needed to develop an actual prioritization mechanism. A set of criteria and weights needs to be agreed on. More importantly, not only physical interventions, but also institutional frameworks and other complementary policies need to be further examined. Currently, the government is preparing a national transport master plan for which this report hopefully provides a lot of useful insights.

This report and data collected under this study revealed some untapped economic opportunities in the transport and other economic sectors. The main challenges and opportunities are summarized in table 7.1.

TABLE 7.1 **Summary of opportunities and challenges**

	OPPORTUNITIES	CHALLENGES
Connectivity	The road network covers the country. Paved roads are well maintained. Connectivity is good around Monrovia and along major corridors from Monrovia to Ganta, Buchanan, and Bo Waterside, where many people live. In these areas, market and port accessibility is good. Approximately 90 percent of the total population lives within 2 hours of a large city. Two-thirds of the total population lives 4 hours from Freeport of Monrovia	Road quality remains a challenge especially in inland areas. Approximately 60 percent of unpaved roads are in poor or very poor condition. Road structures also need to be repaired; 50 percent of bridges and 25 percent of culverts are in poor or very poor condition
		Beyond paved corridors, road connectivity is limited, especially between the north and south, because of poor road conditions
	Cabotage between Monrovia and other ports may have the potential to reduce transport costs dramatically in inland areas such as Lofa County and southeastern regions	Seamless intermodal connection is essential for cabotage. Further assessment is needed for technical and institutional feasibility
Port	Ports are important assets for Liberia, which is a significant importing country. As the economy recovers, it is likely that demand for port operations will increase. Port traffic is heavily concentrated in Freeport of Monrovia, which still seems operationally efficient, perhaps taking advantage of scale economies in port operations	There is an indication that the capacity of Freeport of Monrovia is constrained. Other ports (Buchanan, Greenville, and Harper) may have more potential capacity, but their inland service areas are narrow because of the poor condition of the road network and absence of local large cities
		Economic viability of port operations needs to be verified if cabotage takes place
Rail	Railways are another important asset of the country. Rail transportation has the advantage of bulk, long-haul shipments, possibly including regional freight demand. The Lamco rail line (270 kilometers) has been rehabilitated and is operational. If it were used to connect inland areas around Ganta to Buchanan, transport costs could be reduced by 20–30 percent	The potential effect of rail transport depends on intermodal connectivity, especially at the Port of Buchanan. Institutional arrangements can be complex, including the existing rail concession agreement

continued

TABLE 7.1, *continued*

	OPPORTUNITIES	CHALLENGES
Agriculture	Liberia has fertile land, but productivity is low. Among others, rural access and market accessibility are important to stimulate agricultural production. There is significant correlation between them	Rural accessibility is 41.9 percent, leaving 2.3 million rural people unconnected to the good road network. Approximately 60 percent of unpaved roads are in poor or very poor condition. Significant resources are needed. It is estimated that at least US$850 million would be needed to rehabilitate all poor roads (exclusive of road structures). Strategic prioritization is critical
Fishery	The country has a 570-kilometer-long coastline. Approximately 9,000 crews, including approximately 3,000 foreign fishermen, engage in fishing activities, landing 7,000 tons of fish, which is lower than neighboring countries. Liberia imports fish. There is significant market potential in the region	Among others, rural connectivity from landing sites to markets is missing. Fish are perishable. Of 1,280 kilometers of key market access roads, 1,000 kilometers are currently in fair, poor, or very poor condition and need to be improved and maintained
Agglomeration economies	Liberia is highly urbanized. Approximately 90 percent of the total population lives within 2 hours of a large city or market. Accessibility is particularly high around Monrovia and along the Monrovia-Ganta corridor. Firms are highly concentrated in Monrovia, which reinforces growth of the city because of agglomeration economies. More firms will be located around Monrovia, inviting more investment and generating more jobs	Except for the Monrovia-Ganta corridor, market accessibility, especially to the market of Monrovia, is limited, such as Lofa, Grand Gedeh, Grand Kru, and Maryland Counties, where poverty is higher. It is a challenge to promote growth in urban areas other than Monrovia Monrovia might become more congested. More people and more firms would be located in the city. Long-term urban planning and mass transit development will be required
Regional connectivity and trade	Although road conditions need to be improved, the north-central region around Ganta (Bong and Nimba Counties) is relatively well connected to neighboring countries, especially Guinea and Côte d'Ivoire. There is a possibility to expand regional connectivity and trade, possibly taking advantage of rail connectivity to Buchanan	In general, regional inland connectivity remains low along the Harper-Voinjama corridor. Connectivity to Sierra Leone is especially weak. It is a challenge to stimulate regional trade because all neighboring countries are small and have their own seaports, except for landlocked countries such as Mali and Burkina Faso. Strong political leadership may be needed

Source: World Bank based on data provided by the government of Liberia.

Appendix A
Global Experience of Cabotage

BRAZIL

Short sea shipping (SSS) is a relevant scenario of maritime cabotage in Brazil. SSS covers 8,000 kilometers of coastline and a strong concentration of economic activities along it. Over the past few decades, coastal navigation has increased in Brazil by more than 20 percent a year (figure A.1). This is due to two reasons: first, most of the nation's largest cities and state capitals enjoy access to sea ports; second, activities for long-distance shipping and expansion of cargo handling facilities in the ports have been reoriented.

Currently, there are four companies that undertake most of the SSS activities in Brazil. These are Mercosul Line (Maersk Group), Alliance (Hamburg-Süd Group), Log-In, and Maestra. Altogether these companies operate six dedicated ships for SSS and connect feeder services to the system. As a part of their operational strategy, the companies use smaller vessels for transshipment in ports.

The Brazilian coastal shipping sector involves 36 ports of public administration, three privately managed ports, and 46 private terminals. Whereas, the SSS system has 93 private port terminals and 87 public terminals for utilization.

Salient characteristics of SSS. The main advantages of the SSS system are: managing door-to-door cargo integrity, providing enhanced security, competitive cost, integration with other modes of transport, and frequent services with defined departures and arrivals. The SSS also provides economic benefits such as reduced use of road transport, reduced congestion in port access, lower pollutant emissions in port areas and the consequent decrease in the levels of greenhouse gas emissions in the country. With the entry of new vessels to serve the domestic market, the growth of the indigenous shipbuilding industry has strongly increased.

Compared to maritime transport, road freight door-to-door transport costs less. This is because it is mainly based on the cost of the truck, free use of Brazilian roads, subsidies on diesel fuel, and unregulated working hours for truck drivers. The situation is different for shipping companies. The parameters include cost of capital represented by the vessel, operating costs (insurance, maintenance, crew, food, etc.) considered as fixed whether the ship is operating or not, and travel costs (fuel and port charges) that are mostly not defined by the operator with no subsidies.

Obstacles to SSS. There are general obstacles to develop waterway systems, such as long distances from ports connecting to production centers, inflexibility with the waterway system, slower movement of goods, saturated port infrastructure, and access restrictions from the sea (depth) and land (road and rail). There are more country-specific and policy-related obstacles to the development of SSS in Brazil. On the vessel side, the bunker fuel costs of SSS are about 20 percent more expensive than long-distance navigation. This is because the incidence of taxes for SSS companies accounts for a larger share of their operating costs in Brazil.

The number of ships in operation is limited because of the national restrictions on vessels that are not built in Brazil. To support the development of Merchant Navy and Brazilian naval shipping and repair industry, the Government of Brazil introduced a compensation program from AFRMM (Additional Freight for the Renovation of the Merchant Marine) on freight surcharge for the renewal of the marine market. However, this compensation tends to be delayed because of non-availability of supporting budget. There is also a contractual flaw in the shipbuilding industry in Brazil. Most of the shipbuilding yards do not have the guarantee compliance with the contract. Thus, the construction of boats is often significantly delayed.

Finally, the operating costs of Brazilian vessels are normally higher than flags of convenience vessels. One of the reasons is the high cost of crew social charges: labor costs in Brazil are known to be high, which is reflected in workers' wages. As a result, the development of a cabotage market may be undermined.

Obstacles to seaports. On the port side, SSS is normally given low priority for access to ports and pilotage since the domestic cargo generates smaller revenue from a lower number of vessels compared to deep-sea traffic. Many ports are already congested due to deep-sea traffic. As a result, there are longer waiting times for berthing of bulk solids and liquids for SSS purposes. In addition,

FIGURE A.1

SSS share in the cargo movement in Brazil, 1998–2010

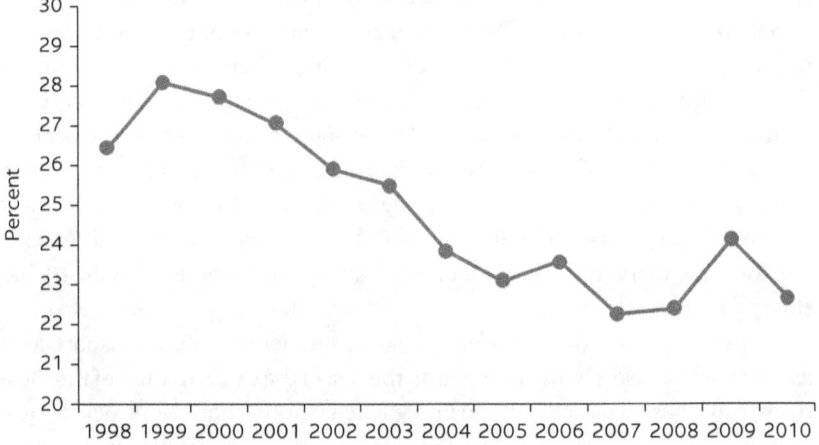

Source: Medina 2011.

many port operations in Brazil are hindered due to the critical condition of the ports and weather events that have occurred in recent years. In 2010, for example, the low level of water in the Amazon River, along with intense winds severely affected port operations. The cost of waiting time for berthing of ships and port expenses for loading and unloading containers also created dissatisfaction over the use of coastal shipping.

As a result of these obstacles, the long-term trend of cabotage use has been declining in recent years. However, there is still potential to (re)develop SSS operations in Brazil. A study (Medina 2011) indicates that SSS companies handled 348,000 TEUs in 2010, while about 1.2 million TEUs of cargo could also have been handled by cabotage but actually were carried by trucks in Brazil. Thus, there is a potential market that is three times larger than the current level.

NIGERIA

In Nigeria, the cabotage law can be characterized as the law that restricts the coastal and inland water trade in a country to vessels flying its national flag. It acts as a protective law that safeguards the interests of local shipping in the carriage of locally generated cargo. Nigeria has a coastline of about 870 km and about 3,000 km of inland waterways. Inland waterways play an important role in the transport of a wide variety of natural resources that the country possesses, such as petroleum, natural gas, tin, columbite, iron ore, coal, zinc, limestone, and lead.

The Coastal and Inland Shipping (Cabotage) Act 2003. Primarily, the purpose of the act was to restrict the use of foreign vessels in domestic coastal trade and promote the development of indigenous tonnage. The provisions referring the act include restrictions and waivers in order to meet lack of domestic capacity, enforcement, and development and maintenance of a Cabotage Vessel Financing Fund amongst others. The Coastal and Inland Shipping (Cabotage) Act 2003 has a broad definition of the word cabotage that is used interchangeably with coastal trade. Cabotage under the act covers:

- Carriage by sea of goods and passengers from one coastal or inland point, which could be ports, jetties, piers etc., to another point located within Nigeria;
- Carriage of goods and passengers by sea in relation to the exploration, exploitation or transportation of natural resources whether offshore or within the inland and coastal waters;
- Carriage of goods and passengers on water or underwater (sub-sea) installations;
- Carriage of goods and passengers originating from a point in Nigeria intended for Nigeria but transiting through another country then back to Nigeria for discharge;
- Operation by vessel of any other marine transportation activity of a commercial nature in Nigerian waters that includes towage, pilotage, dredging, salvage, bunkering etc. within its territory.

Nigerian Maritime Administration and Safety Agency (NIMASA). NIMASA, formerly the Nigerian Maritime Authority (NMA), acts as a regulatory authority for the implementation and enforcement of cabotage in Nigeria.

The Cabotage Regime. The Cabotage Regime under the Cabotage Act 2003 indicates:

- Cabotage vessels must be wholly owned by Nigerian citizens;
- Cabotage vessels must be manned by Nigerian citizens;
- Cabotage vessels must be registered by Nigerians;
- Cabotage vessels must be built at Nigerian shipyards.

The act follows that in the event of non-availability of certain local capacity, three out of four parameters can be waived. It insists that shipping companies be incorporated by the Corporate Affairs Commission. The Cabotage Act preserves the rights of foreign investors under the Nigerian Investment Promotion Commission Act by establishing a Special Register for cabotage (fully foreign-owned vessel) for foreign-owned vessels engaged in cabotage trade.

The act further provides that a tug or vessel not wholly owned by a Nigerian citizen shall not tow any vessel from or into any port or point in Nigerian waters or tow any vessel carrying any substance whatsoever, whether of value or not or any dredge material and whether or not it has commercial value from a port or point within Nigerian waters. The restriction does not preclude a foreign vessel from rendering assistance to persons, vessels or aircraft in danger or distress in Nigerian waters thereby acknowledging the Salvage Convention and International Customary Laws for vessels under distress.

Waivers. The act gives the Minister of Transport the power to allow foreign vessels to participate in cabotage trade as long as there is no capacity on the part of Nigerians. The waivers considered in the act are as under:

- Waiver of the requirement that the vessel be wholly Nigerian-owned;
- Waiver of the requirement that the vessel be wholly manned by Nigerian citizens;
- Waiver of the requirement that the vessel be built in Nigeria.

Challenges of cabotage law in Nigeria. Since cabotage law came into force in Nigeria on May 1, 2004, numerous challenges have bedeviled its effective implementation and enforcement. First, as there is presently insufficient Nigerian fleet to cater to the demand for transportation, the conditions for foreign firms to obtain a waiver are less challenging to engage in cabotage in Nigeria. Thus, with the waiver, the bulk of the indigenous vessel holders' responsibilities have been shifted to the foreigners. This had made the Cabotage Act ineffective and at the same time defeating its purpose from the exceptions.

Second, the ports' infrastructure facilities are not on par with international standards and are commercially unfriendly. While high tariffs are charged, the serviceability of ports is poor. Furthermore, the high cost of enforcement and monitoring is a big challenge since facilities and equipment for enforcement are insufficient with no capacity to handle operations.

A cursory look at the significant role shipping plays in Nigeria's economy shows that it is imperative for the government to assist in the process. This assistance can be in the form of funds for industry stakeholders to acquire ships and become self-sufficient.

Nigeria's Cabotage Act has been discussed around the world, especially in the United States and Indonesia. In Nigeria, it serves to protect citizens' interests. Efficient enforcement of the act will have economic benefits for Nigeria that outweigh the challenges presented by its implementation and monitoring.

REFERENCE

Medina, Afonso Celso. 2011. "Short Sea Shipping in Brazil: Potential and Policy Implications." IAME Conference, October 28.

Appendix B
Public-Private Partnership Framework and Case Studies in Liberia

GOVERNMENT ENTITIES GOVERNING THE LEGAL FRAMEWORK

The National Bureau of Concessions (NBC) was established by NBC Act on September 23, 2011, in order to provide the governance framework necessary to coordinate the post-concession award process. This includes monitoring, evaluating, and reporting as a basis for enforcing (in cooperation with relevant ministries) concessionaires' and the government of Liberia's compliance with the obligations contained in the agreements. The bureau monitors and evaluates compliance with concession agreements in collaboration with concession granting entities.

The Public Procurement and Concessions Commission is a public autonomous institution established by a 2005 Act of the Legislature to ensure the economic and efficient use of public funds in public procurement, and that public procurement and concessions (PPC) processes are conducted in a fair, transparent, and non-discriminatory manner. With respect to the PPC Act, the following provisions for entities have been defined for the procurement and concession process:

- **Procurement and concession entities.** Different procurement or concession entities are formed with the division of responsibilities at different levels of the process
- **A procurement entity** forms a procurement committee along with a bid evaluation panel to monitor and review the procurement process
- **A concession entity** proposes an entity concession committee for the review of the concessions along with a bid evaluation panel
- An **Inter-Ministerial Concessions Committee (IMCC)** is formed for a specific concession to evaluate and monitor the concession at different levels. The IMCC is defined to comprise the following members:
  a. The chairperson of the National Investment Commission
  b. The Minister of Justice

c. The Minister of Finance
d. The Minister of Labor
e. The Minister of Planning and Economic Affairs
f. The Minister of Internal Affairs
g. Two ministers appointed by the president representing the sectors of concession
h. The head of the concession entity.

The Liberia Extractive Industries Transparency Initiative (LEITI): With the Public Procurement Concession Commission (PPCC) in place, Liberia adopted the Extractive Industries Transparency Initiative best practices as a candidate in 2008 and became the first African country, and the second globally, to become EITI compliant in 2009. LEITI was established by an Act of the Legislature in July 2009 as an autonomous agency that promotes revenue transparency and accountability from the extractive sectors. LEITI is a multi-stakeholder process, bringing together the government of Liberia, civil society, and investors in the extractive sectors.

The relevant sector ministries work closely with the National Investment Commission (NIC) to identify investors and further establish an IMCC to review, negotiate, and present a concession agreement. Once a concession agreement has been signed and ratified, the ministries work in consultation with the NBC to:

- monitor and evaluate compliance with concession agreements in collaboration with concession granting entities
- provide technical assistance to concession entities involved with the implementation of concessions in compliance with the PPC Act.

As per LEITI's annual report, the following legal framework governing the development of different sectors have been defined.[1]

Mining Sector

The Ministry of Lands, Mines and Energy (MLME) is the government agency that is responsible for the administration of the mineral sector, including granting mining licenses. It has statutory oversight of the energy, land, minerals, and water sectors. It focuses on development of the regulatory reform for a modern, state-of-the-art concession framework for mineral deposits in order to maximize sustainable contributions of mining to the national economy. The sector is regulated by the Mining and Minerals Law of 2000. The Minerals Policy of Liberia was created in March 2010 to complement the Mining and Minerals Law. Exports and imports of rough diamonds are overseen by the Government Diamond Office (GDO) within the MLME and by the Bureau of Customs and Excise.

Energy Sector

The MLME regulates the oil and gas industry while the **National Oil Company of Liberia (NOCAL)**, which was set up in 2000 by the NOCAL Act 2000 and 2002 Petroleum Law, administers and controls the rights, title, and interest in oil and gas deposits and reserves in the Liberian territory and also facilitates the development of the oil and gas industry in Liberia. The NOCAL is also mandated to grant exploration licenses and negotiate on behalf of the government in all petroleum-related contracts. NOCAL chairs the **Hydrocarbon Technical Committee (HTC)**—the inter-ministerial body created by the 2002 Petroleum Law that is empowered to negotiate all contracts. The Hydrocarbons Law 2002 and the National Petroleum Policy of 2012 governs with the regulations for the energy sector.

Agriculture Sector

The Ministry of Agriculture (MoA) is responsible for the leadership and overall development of the agricultural sector. It does so by ensuring that an effective organizational structure is put in place and is manned by staff capable of planning, coordinating, implementing, monitoring, and periodically evaluating agricultural development programs.

Forestry Sector

The Forestry Development Authority (FDA) is responsible for development of the forestry sector. The following are the specific regulations that apply to the forestry sector:

- Act creating the FDA of 1976
- National Forestry Reform Law of 2006
- Forestry Core Regulations—FDA Ten Core Regulations (effective September 2007)
- Act to Establish the Community Rights Law With Respect to Forest Lands of 2009
- FDA Regulations to the Community Rights Law with Respect to Forest Lands, July 2011
- Guidelines for Forest Management Planning in Liberia
- National Forest Management Strategy, 2007.

Forestry sector contracts differ depending upon the area and scope of work and have been categorized as:

- **Forest Management Contract (FMC):** It is granted to forest concessionaires and covers an operational area ranging between 50,000 and 400,000 hectares, excluding private land. The duration of this contract is **25 years**
- **Timber Sale Contract (TSC):** It is granted to forest concessionaires and covers an operational area not exceeding 5,000 hectares, excluding private land. The duration of this contract is **3 years**
- **Private Use Permit (PUP):** It is granted to private land owners (individual, group, and community) for the purpose of extracting wood. However, due to allegations of misrepresentations and abuses in implementing Liberia's National Forestry Reform Law in handling PUPs, the government has suspended all PUP operations
- **Forest Use Permit (FUP):** It is issued for small-scale forest exploitation, research, NTFP activities or other uses with no details on land area or type of land ownership
- **Community Forest Management Agreement (CFMA):** It is issued to communities for the purpose of community-based forest management and covers an operational area of less than 50 hectares.

PROCUREMENT LAWS

The procurement law for concession contracts of Liberia is PPC Act, 2005 and its subsequent amendments for the procurement of goods, works and services. The act is applicable to all executive agencies, including government ministries, commissions, bureaus, departments and all agencies of the government of Liberia. However, the act is not applicable for, *inter alia*, the following: international agreements concluded between the government of Liberia and other countries or international organizations for general or specific projects where these agreements provide for specified procurement rules and procedures.

Procurement Methods

The PPCC has defined the threshold ceiling of estimated contract prices for procurement contracts for each method for goods, works, and services. The different procurement methods defined by the act are categorized as follows:

Open Competitive Bidding: This method is adopted for complex nature of the goods, works, and services to elicit competitive bids, which may include a pre-qualification or post-qualification procedure.

National Competitive Bidding: This method is adopted when only domestic suppliers or contractors are likely to be interested in submitting bids and where the area falls within the economy.

International Competitive Bidding: This method of procurement is adopted when the estimated contract price is higher than the ceiling threshold established by regulations or the project requires international expertise, technology or capital outlay.

Restrictive Bidding: This method is adopted when the goods, works or services are only available from a limited number of bidders.

Request for Proposal: This method is used for the procurement of consultant services.

Request for Quotations: This method is adopted when the procurement is for readily available commercially standard goods or small works or services for a contract that is not more than 12 months.

Sole Source: This method is permitted only when one supplier has the exclusive right to manufacture the goods, carry out the works or perform the services to be procured and no suitable alternative is available or in case of emergency.

Further, the final selection on the basis for assessment has been divided into the following:

Quality and Cost-Based Selection: One of the following is adopted for the selection of a successful proposal:

- **Quality and Cost-Based Selection (QCBS):** A balancing of the technical quality of the proposal, the consultant's relevant experience, work methodology, and the price of the proposal is used when the estimated contract price exceeds the threshold established by PPCC regulations
- **Fixed-Budget Selection (FBS):** The quality of the technical proposal submitted within a predetermined fixed budget. The consultant that submits the highest-ranked technical proposal within the predetermined fixed budget shall be selected

- **Least-Cost Selection (LCS):** The quality of the technical proposals having met a minimum set of criteria disclosed in the request for proposals and then with the lowest price
- **Consultant's Qualification Selection (CQS):** For smaller assignments on the basis of best qualification and experience.

Based on Quality: When the services are of an exceptionally complex nature or likely to have a considerable impact on future projects, the consultant may be selected exclusively on the basis of the technical quality of the proposal; the use of which method shall be approved by the procurement committee subject to the approval of the commission.

PPC Schedule of Thresholds

According to the **PPC Schedule of Thresholds**, the ceiling for procurement as estimated contract prices is divided as follows:[2]

International Open Competitive Bidding and National Open Competitive Bidding:

- Procurement of goods, US$500,000
- Procurement of services, US$200,000
- Procurement of works, US$1,000,000

Request for Quotations (RFQ):

- Procurement of goods, US$10,000
- Procurement of services, US$10,000
- Procurement of works, US$30,000

Restricted Bidding:

- Procurement of goods, US$50,000
- Procurement of services, US$20,000
- Procurement of works, US$100,000

Sole Source Procurement: Contract estimated price exceeds US$100,000
Non-Consulting Services: Estimated contract price exceeds US$100,000
Lease-Cost Selection: US$100,000.

Margin of Preference

As per Section 45 and Regulation 21 of the Act, a margin of preference clause has been included for the benefit of Liberian businesses ensuring enhanced participation and partnerships during the procurement or concession process. The general objective of the margin of preference is to provide an opportunity to Liberian and domestic businesses to have a competitive edge in procurement (works, services, and goods), investment loan, and other business activities.

The margin of preference defined by the Act for the different methods are:

Consultancy Services-EOI:

- Domestic business: 10 percent
- Liberian business: 20 percent

Consultancy and Non-Consultancy Services—Financial Evaluation:

- Domestic business: 10 percent
- Liberian business: 20 percent

Goods manufactured with less than 30 percent of inputs imported:

- Domestic business: 10 percent
- Liberian business: 50 percent

Goods manufactured with more than 30 percent of inputs imported:

- Domestic business: 10 percent
- Liberian business: 30 percent

Works:

- Domestic businesses: 2 percent
- Liberian businesses: 10 percent

CONCESSION AGREEMENTS

The act has a separate part (Part VI) for specific procedures for processing concession agreements. As per Section 73 of Part VI of the act, concession is defined as the following: **"Concession"** means the granting of an interest in a public asset by the government or its agency to a private sector entity for a specified period during which the asset may be operated, managed, utilized or improved by the private sector entity that pays fees or royalties on the condition that the government retains its overall interest in the asset and that the asset will revert to the government or agency at a determined time.

Determination of Concession Objectives

Determination of the specific objectives of a concession shall be arrived at in consultation with all key stakeholder entities, including, but not limited to:

(1). The Ministry of Finance
(2). The Ministry for Planning and Economic Affairs
(3). The National Investment Commission
(4). The Ministry of Justice
(5). The Ministry of Labor
(6). The Ministry of Internal Affairs
(7). Agencies with direct relevance to the proposed concession.

Implementation of the Concession Process

As per the PPC Act, implementation of the concession shall include the following:

a) Identification and certification for concessions
b) Planning of the process for concession agreements
c) Preparation of concession bid documents
d) Invitation and evaluation of bids, negotiations, and signing of concession agreements
e) Implementation, supervision, and monitoring of concession agreements.

The PPC Act lays down detailed procedures for procurement as well implementation of the concession. As per the act, the following activities/steps are required to be followed for procurement of a concession (table B.1).

TABLE B.1 **Procurement steps by PPC act**

	ACTIVITY
1.	Submission of request for concession certificate to the Ministry for Planning and Economic Affairs
2.	Issuance of concession certificate by the Ministry for Planning and Economic Affairs
3.	Formation of Inter-Ministerial Concession Committee (IMCC)
4.	Commencement of public consultation
5.	Completion of public consultation
6.	Preparation of procurement plan
7.	Submission of procurement plan to IMCC and the commission
8.	Approval of procurement plan by IMCC and the commissions
9.	Submission of pre-qualification documents and bidding documents to IMCC and the commission
10.	Approval of pre-qualification documents by IMCC and the commission
11.	Issuance of pre-qualification documents
12.	Receipt of pre-qualification documents
13.	Evaluation of pre-qualification documents and issuance of RFP to shortlisted applicants
14.	Receipt of bids
15.	Evaluation of bids and selection of preferred bidders

CASE STUDY I—MARYLAND OIL PALM PLANTATION

A concession agreement was signed between the government of Liberia and Maryland Oil Palm Plantation Inc. on August 2, 2011. The key terms and conditions of the concession included the following:.

Concession Area

The area granted under this concession in the Decoris Oil Palm Plantation is:

- 8,800 hectares concession area
- Additional area of 6,400 acres for out-growers program.

Concession Period

- Term of the concession—concession period: 25 years
- Renewal/extension of the term: Additional 10 years
- Rights of the concessionaire.

Rights of the Concessionaire

The rights of the concessionaire under this concession included the following:

- Production of oil palm products
- Use and sale of oil palm products
- Export of oil palm products
- Use and sale of carbon rights of the concession area.

Payments

- Upfront payment: US$3,100,000
- Surface Rental Fee: Annual payment of US$2 per acre within the developed area and US$1 per acre of undeveloped land within the concession area
- Community Development Contribution: Annual contribution of US$5 per hectare within the developed area to a community development fund established for development purposes
- Oil Palm Development Fund: Contribution of one percent of its annual gross sales of oil palm products, processed oil palm, and oil palm byproducts to the Oil Palm Development Fund.

Investment

- The concessionaire had to make a total investment of US$64 million of which US$48 million was for the development of the concession area through plantation, including land preparation cost, and US$16 million for the out-growers program for the palm plantation.

Monitoring and Evaluation

- The investments and payments are monitored by the National Investment Commission and Ministry of Finance.
- The periodic operational financial reports are required to be submitted by the concessionaire to the MoA and Ministry of Finance.

Infrastructure Provisions

- **Concession Area:** The concession agreement gives an exclusive right to the concessionaire to construct, install, maintain, and/or repair, at its own expense, infrastructure within the concession area with the prior approval of the government.
- **Outside the Concession Area:** The concessionaire has a right to, at its own expense, construct and establish infrastructure, subject to prior written approval from the government.
- All highways and roadways constructed pursuant to this shall, upon completion, become public property. However, that investor shall have the right to use such highways and roadways without charge or the imposition of taxes and duties.

Risk Allocation

- According to the concession, the investor shall bear the cost of and pay for all the resettlement expenses up to a maximum of US$200 per hectare of land that requires resettlement and the government will bear the cost and pay for resettlement expenses that exceed US$200 per hectare of land that requires resettlement, which will be done by the resettlement commission.

Termination

- During termination, the winding up commission was constituted for settlement of operations.

Termination Payment and Disposition of Assets

- According to the terms and conditions, in case of termination due to default by the government, the government shall compensate the investor for the fair market value of the loss of benefit of the concession agreement and the use of the concession area, including the use of the non-moveable assets as damages.
- In case of movable assets, the government has the right and the first option to purchase the assets at fair market value.

CASE STUDY II: CHINA UNION MINING CO. LTD. AND CHINA-UNION INVESTMENT BONG MINES CO. LTD

A concession agreement was signed between the government of Liberia, China Union Mining Co. Ltd., and China-Union Investment Bong Mines Co. Ltd. in January of 2009. The key terms and conditions of the concession included the following:

Concession Period: Term of the Concession—Concession Period: 25 years

Rights of the Concessionaire

- Commercial exploitation of minerals found in the concession area, which includes design, construction, installation, fabrication, operation, maintenance, and repair of the mining plant, infrastructure and any other equipment, and the mining processing, stockpiling, transportation, export, and sale of such minerals.

Total Concession Area: 153,000 acres
- Initial Concession Area: Approximately 59,000 acres
- Additional Concession Area: 94,000 acres.

Payments

- **Royalty:** The royalty rate for shipment or sale of iron ore was defined as follows on the basis of index price which if:
  - Equal to US$100 per metric ton (MT) or less = 3.25%
  - Greater than US$100 per MT or less than US$125 per MT = 3.5%
  - Greater than US$125 per MT and less than US$150 per MT = 4.0%
  - US$150 per MT or more = 4.5%.
- **Surface Rental:** Surface rent of concession area was defined as:
  - US$100,000 per year for 10 years
  - US$250,000 per year for next 15 years.
- **Upfront Payment:** Concessionaire shall pay the government US$40,000,000 as upfront payment.
- **Mineral Development and Research Fund:** One-time payment to the government of US$50,000.
- **Scientific Research Fund:** The concessionaire shall also make an annual contribution of US$100,000.

Infrastructure Provisions: Transportation

- The concessionaire has the right to develop, use, operate, and maintain the railway linking the mines to the port facility and also has the right to develop, use, operate, and maintain the port facilities subject to third-party rights.

- The government may grant third-party use of excess capacity of the rail and port facilities provided that it does not interfere with the operations of the concessionaire. The technical and commercial terms of such third-party use shall be mutually agreed between the government and the concessionaire.
- Currently, Monrovia to Bong Mines railway track is associated with China Union (80 km).

Infrastructure Provisions: Electricity

- Electricity Generation and Transmission: The concessionaire is entitled to provide the installation of electric generating capacity for conducting operations in Liberia for infrastructure:
  (a) Construction of a heavy oil power plant
  (b) Development of a hydroelectric power plant with a generation capacity of 130 MW
  (c) Purchase of another 100 MW of power from other hydroelectric power plants.

CASE STUDY III: FOREST DEVELOPMENT AUTHORITY AND ATLANTIC RESOURCES LIMITED

An FMC was signed between the FDA and Atlantic Resources in 2009. The general terms of this contract consisted of the following:

Concession Area: 119,344 hectares
Concession Period: 25 years.

Rights of the Concessionaire

- The right of the concessionaire was defined to harvest timber in the contract area.

Payments

- **Land Rental:** US$8.90 per hectare payable annually
- **Initial Performance Bond:** US$250,000
- **Stumpage Fees:** As per Regulation 107-07 of the FDA
- **Log Export Fee:** As per Regulation 107-07 of the FDA
- **Minimum Expenditure for Processing Facilities (Sawmill and Plywood Mill):** US$22,200,000.

CASE STUDY IV: CONCESSIONS IN TRANSPORTATION SECTOR

The government of Liberia is now focusing on the development of transportation sectors through concessions. In 2011, the **National Port Authority (NPA)** entered into a concession with APM Terminals for the Freeport of Monrovia with a systematic process. The process began with an assessment of the legal and regulatory framework and of the various public-private partnership (PPP) options worth considering. A market consultation exercise was then carried out by a team of international consultants and government officials. The EOI and RFP process was followed through competitive bidding mode of procurement. The key features of the concessions were as follows:

Concession Period: 25 years
Mode: Rehabilitate, operate, and transfer
Investment: The concessionaire had to invest US$120 million over the course of the PPP where the concessionaire shall have the following responsibilities:

- reconstruction of the marginal wharf
- development of the container and general cargo terminal
- provision of container and general cargo operations
- provision of marine services (pilotage, towage, mooring, and unmooring).

Payments: The payments by the concessionaire included:

- Fixed annual lease fee
- Percentage of service rate revenue.

During 2016–17, concessions by Liberia Airport Authority for development of a cargo facility and by NPA for development of the Port of Greenville have been under consideration and the process is currently ongoing. The procurement process of the first PPP concession in the transport sector (road) in Liberia, development of Ganta-Tappita road, is also currently ongoing.

NOTES

1. http://www.leiti.org.lr/uploads/2/1/5/6/21569928/leiti_2014-2015_eiti_final_report_18-08-2016-signed.pdf.
2. http://www.ppcc.gov.lr/content.php?sub=67&related=1&third=67&pg=sp.

www.ingramcontent.com/pod-product-compliance
Lightning Source LLC
Chambersburg PA
CBHW081422230426
43668CB00016B/2321